IBM Lotus Notes Guide

A practical, hands-on user guide with time-saving tips and comprehensive instructions for using Lotus Notes effectively and efficiently

Karen Hooper

PUBLISHING

BIRMINGHAM - MUMBAI

IBM Lotus Notes 8.5 User Guide

First published: September 2010

Production Reference: 2300810

Published by Packt Publishing Ltd.
32 Lincoln Road
Olton
Birmingham, B27 6PA, UK

ISBN 978-1-849680-20-2

www.packtpub.com

Cover Image by Sandeep Babu (sandyjb@gmail.com)

Credits

Author
Karen Hooper

Reviewers
Susan Bulloch

Karen Hobert

Mary Beth Raven

Kathy Staples

Acquisition Editor
Kerry George

Development Editor
Dhwani Devater

Technical Editor
Gaurav Datar

Indexer
Rekha Nair

Editorial Team Leader
Gagandeep Singh

Project Team Leader
Priya Mukherji

Project Coordinator
Zainab Bagasrawala

Proofreader
Lynda Sliwoski

Graphics
Nilesh Mohite

Production Coordinator
Kruthika Bangera

Cover Work
Kruthika Bangera

Foreword

You are in possession of a valuable resource—Karen Hooper's IBM Lotus Notes 8.5 User Guide. Within the chapters of this book, you will find step-by-step instructions, examples, and tips on how to make the best use of your Lotus Notes 8.5 environment. New Lotus Notes users and old pros alike will find ideas and reinforcements in Karen's careful and detailed examination of Notes from the end-user perspective.

Lotus Notes 8 represents the realization of a key vision and evolution for Notes users. Several years before the current version's release, IBM recognized the need to modernize the Lotus Notes client environment. Under the codename of Hannover, IBM architects, engineers, and usability experts pursued the future vision for Lotus Notes.

The four main principles of the Notes 8 release were world-class usability, an open architecture, integration with other IBM Lotus software, and innovation. During the development phase of the Notes 8 project, IBM engineers conducted over 1000 usability test site visits, and surveyed various focus groups, learning what end users expected from the best messaging and collaboration environment in the market. They blended best-in-class features with innovative new capabilities, direct from IBM Labs. The result was the product you use, or, are considering today—a remarkable step forward for Lotus Notes.

Since the initial release of Notes 8, IBM engineers have adopted an agile development approach, adding incremental improvements to Notes in frequent releases. This book focuses on Notes 8.5, first released in 2009. While IBM continues to invent the future, notably with its new Project Vulcan vision for the next decade of Notes, you can be confident of having the best tool for corporate collaboration today.

In this book, you will find Karen's passion played out on every page. I have met Karen in person during my annual visits to Australia, and enjoyed sharing perspectives about Notes and collaboration with her for the last several years. As someone whose firm is named Dr Notes, Karen clearly has confidence in her abilities and understands the best practices with regards to the use of Lotus Notes, which you will see clearly on display in this book.

In the IBM Lotus Notes 8.5 User Guide, Karen Hooper takes you through the entire spectrum of end-user capabilities. The first chapter explains the basics, with subsequent chapters jumping right into the deeper waters to explore more powerful capabilities. I am particularly pleased with the depth of exploration of the integrated IBM Lotus Sametime capabilities; many organizations have moved far beyond "why do we need chat?" to full understanding of integrated presence, whiteboarding, and even synchronous voice services. There are full chapters dedicated to the extensibility and openness of the Notes 8.5 environment, including the RSS feeds service, and most importantly, sidebar widgets. In Chapter 6, users will find tools and tips that have often been under-utilized in typical Notes environments, but are extremely useful and powerful. Finally, users will benefit from exploring the chapter on the integrated productivity suite, IBM Lotus Symphony, as an opportunity and alternative to expensive office productivity tools.

In addition to the excellent materials in this book, I would also encourage you to check out a full range of end-user assistance tools available on IBM's website. Visit `http://www.ibm.com/developerworks/lotus/notes` for a wiki full of additional tutorials, examples, plugins, and more. While there, you can visit forums and community websites, and connect to Lotus Notes users and advocates around the world.

My best wishes for your continued success, and congratulations to Karen on a job well done.

—Ed Brill
Director, Lotus Notes Product Management
IBM Corporation
Chicago, USA
Twitter: @edbrill

About the Author

Karen Hooper is an IBM Certified Instructor in both System Administration and Development. Karen and her husband Steve own and manage Dr Notes Solutions, a Premier IBM Business Partner and IBM Authorized Training Partner, based in Australia.

Karen has over 13 years of experience with Lotus Notes and Domino, from version 4 to 8.5.1. Karen has been involved in several major upgrade projects and company-wide training initiatives. She has been responsible for customizing and producing end user and help desk training material for several organizations. End user training is a passion for Karen as she believes an investment in training will always give a return to both the individual and the organization. Karen is also a technical instructor in both Domino System Administration and Development. Her passion is to empower people so that they increase their productivity and use the tools available to them. Karen has seen thousands of people benefit from her style of training.

Karen lives in a beautiful bayside suburb of Melbourne, Australia with her husband Steve. They are blessed with two children, Zac and Zoe, and two Cavoodles, Jess and Bella.

If you wish to contact Karen, her e-mail ID is `Karen.Hooper@drnotes.com.au`.

There are so many people I need to thank for helping me bring this book into reality. First and foremost is my husband Steve who is the love of my life and the "above all else Karen do your book" disciplinarian! I had the wonderful joy of giving birth to our beautiful little daughter Zoe Grace during the writing of this book and at times found it incredibly tough to meet the deadlines. If it wasn't for Steve it would not have happened. I need to also thank Zac, the other gorgeous man in my life. Thank you for helping me and praying for me to get the book done. Your encouragement really helped — plus putting out the rubbish and cleaning up the kitchen :). To the guys at Dr Notes, you all inspire me, you guys simply all rock. Thank you to the guys at Packt — Kerry, Zainab, Dhwani, and Gaurav — you did well to put up with me and my hormones. A big thank you to Ed Brill for recommending me to Packt — it was a highlight in my career. Also a big thank you to Mary Beth Raven, Karen Hobert, and Kathy Staples for their invaluable input. All of you are incredibly busy and I appreciated and was honored with you taking the time to review this book. I can only hope that this book represents Lotus Notes in its best light; I believe in the product and the people behind it.

About the Reviewers

Susan Bulloch has worked for IBM Lotus Software for 10 years in software support and development positions. Susan currently works as a Support Engineer on the Lotus Products SWAT Team, supporting the entire Lotus product line, specializing in Lotus Notes and Domino. She has worked with Lotus Notes and Domino since 1992 as an administrator, instructor, developer, and architect in the banking and utility industries. Susan has a Bachelor's degree in engineering and a Master's degree in Information Technology. She holds certifications in all current Lotus Notes and Domino product releases, and is actively involved in quality testing Beta versions of new IBM products. Susan is a frequent speaker at technical conferences, including Lotusphere, the View Admin conferences, and at regional user group conferences worldwide.

Karen Hobert is a Principal Analyst at Top Dog—an independent IT research analysis and consulting firm based in Los Angeles, CA. Karen is an enterprise-focused information technology research analyst, programmer, consultant, and educator with expertise in communication, collaboration, social software, content management, and enterprise data management technologies. She is also the author of courses and workshops on web-based business process applications and is a founding member of the Collaborative Strategy Guild.

Mary Beth Raven leads the user experience design team for Lotus Notes. She joined the Notes team in 2005 and started working on Lotus Notes 8. Prior to that, she worked on the user experience design of five versions of Lotus Sametime. Mary Beth has worked on user experience design at IBM, FTP software, and Digital Equipment Corporation. She has a Ph.D. in Rhetoric and Communication from Rensselaer Polytechnic Institute in Troy, NY, U.S.A.

Kathy Staples has over 20 years of experience in the IT Industry and has been in many roles, including helpdesk officer, software developer, network engineer/administrator, and technical sales. Kathy has spent the last 10 years with IBM in a technical sales role for Lotus Software, which has included a short period working with the Linux team to develop and maintain part of the Linux Kernel. Kathy has gained full certification in a number of disciplines, those being Novell, Microsoft, and Lotus.

Table of Contents

Preface

Lotus Notes is quite a number of "things", including e-mail, calendar, To Dos (tasks), chat, RSS Feeder, an applications platform, and more. Being able to master all these aspects is made simple with this exciting user guide. Many of us will use Lotus Notes for most of our working day; and being able to use it more efficiently is a gain in our hectic work life. Many of us want to use tools and features to save time, but often we are unsure of how to master those tools and features. This book offers a guide with explanations and clear instructions with explicit screenshots.

What this book covers

Chapter 1, First Impressions (The Client Interface), explores and explains what we first see and how we work with what we see when we open Lotus Notes.

Chapter 2, To Chat or Not to Chat: Lotus Sametime, covers the benefits and features of Lotus Sametime, which is a built-in chat and presence-awareness tool.

Chapter 3, Feeds, delves into what feeds are and how to set them up in Lotus Notes.

Chapter 4, Working with Widgets, discusses Widgets and Live Text and explains their use in Lotus Notes.

Chapter 5, Mastering Lotus Notes Mail, helps us understand mail in more detail.

Chapter 6, Lotus Notes Mail Tools, focuses on the advanced features available in Mail and how we can best utilize them to assist us in being efficient with mail management.

Chapter 7, Managing Contacts, explores how to organize, add, import, export, and manage contacts and groups (mailing or distribution lists).

Chapter 8, Calendar and To Dos, explores the calendar and To Dos in depth.

Chapter 9, Working with Lotus Notes Applications, explores the Lotus Notes application with real-world examples.

Chapter 10, Working Remotely (Replication/Synchronization), explores the benefits of working remotely in Lotus Notes and how to do so.

Chapter 11, Symphony, discusses IBM's award-winning office productivity software, Lotus Symphony, which allows us to create documents, spreadsheets, presentations, and even has a PDF creator.

What you need for this book

Lotus Notes is a multiplatform client application and is available in several languages. In this book, we have specifically covered the attributes of Lotus Notes 8.5 English client installed on a Windows operating system. As it is a client-server application, it works in conjunction with a Domino server. When we install and configure the client software, it will prompt us for our user name and home server. If we are performing these steps, we need to make sure we have these details, or we can contact our IT Department to determine what is required.

Who this book is for

This book is suitable for anyone who uses Lotus Notes, from beginners to seasoned professionals who have used it for years. Often we are creatures of habit, even if those habits are the long way around of doing things. This book aims to cover the features and tools that enable us to work smarter. Also, there are significant changes from the earlier versions of Lotus Notes to the current version of 8.5. This book covers the new features in detail so that we will be able to take advantage of them as well; it also covers key features from earlier versions that have stood the test of time.

Conventions

In this book, you will find a number of styles of text that distinguish between different kinds of information. Here are some examples of these styles, and an explanation of their meaning.

New terms and **important words** are shown in bold. Words that you see on the screen, in menus or dialog boxes for example, appear in our text like this: "Open Mail and click on the **More** button in the action bar at the top of the messages."

[ Warnings or important notes appear in a box like this.]

[Tips and tricks appear like this.]

Reader feedback

Feedback from our readers is always welcome. Let us know what you think about this book—what you liked or may have disliked. Reader feedback is important for us to develop titles that you really get the most out of.

To send us general feedback, simply drop an e-mail to feedback@packtpub.com, and mention the book title in the subject of your message.

If there is a book that you need and would like to see us publish, please send us a note in the **SUGGEST A TITLE** form on www.packtpub.com or e-mail suggest@packtpub.com.

If there is a topic that you have expertise in and you are interested in either writing or contributing to a book, see our author guide on www.packtpub.com/authors.

Customer support

Now that you are the proud owner of a Packt book, we have a number of things to help you to get the most from your purchase.

Errata

Although we have taken every care to ensure the accuracy of our contents, mistakes do happen. If you find a mistake in one of our books—maybe a mistake in text or code—we would be grateful if you would report this to us. By doing so, you can save other readers from frustration, and help us to improve subsequent versions of this book. If you find any errata, please report them by visiting http://www.packtpub.com/support, selecting your book, clicking on the errata submission form link, and entering the details of your errata. Once your errata are verified, your submission will be accepted and the errata added to any list of existing errata. Any existing errata can be viewed by selecting your title from http://www.packtpub.com/support.

Piracy

Piracy of copyrighted material on the Internet is an ongoing problem across all media. At Packt, we take the protection of our copyright and licenses very seriously. If you come across any illegal copies of our works in any form on the Internet, please provide us with the location address or website name immediately so that we can pursue a remedy.

Please contact us at copyright@packtpub.com with a link to the suspected pirated material.

We appreciate your help in protecting our authors, and our ability to bring you valuable content.

Questions

You can contact us at questions@packtpub.com if you are having a problem with any aspect of the book, and we will do our best to address it.

First Impressions (The Client Interface)

1

First impressions always count and, when you start Lotus Notes, there is no exception. You might notice that Lotus Notes is much more than just e-mail! There are many feature-rich tools available—for example, there is a free office suite application called **Lotus Symphony** that can be used as an alternative to Microsoft Office for those who just need the basics with an office suite. You will see the ability to create documents, spreadsheets, and presentations if Symphony is selected while installing Lotus Notes. You can also export each of those documents to PDF, HTML, or JPEG format if required.

Lotus Notes also has a Notebook application. This application allows you to create notes that can include pictures, attachments, ideas, and so on. It is a great place to store information that is just for you. It also has an inbuilt chat and presence capability called Sametime, along with an inbuilt RSS feed reader, a Widget panel, calendaring and scheduling capabilities, and applications if your organization has developed any or purchased them.

In this chapter we will focus on the client and will explore the following:

- Starting and shutting down Lotus Notes
- Open List
- Thumbnails
- Home Page
- Shortcuts
- Window tabs
- Toolbars
- Sidebar
- Lotus Notes Browser
- Preferences

Starting Lotus Notes—start your engines

Starting Lotus Notes is similar to starting any application on your computer; simply go to **Start | Programs | Lotus Notes**. You may also have a shortcut to Lotus Notes in your taskbar or on your desktop.

Password prompt

As Lotus Notes is starting up, in most cases we will be prompted for a password. Lotus Notes is a very secure program; it requires us to verify that we are who we say we are, the same as when we use our PIN number with our ATM card. There are variations that can occur with the security within Lotus Notes in some organizations. Lotus Notes may start without a password prompt but be assured the security is still just as strong.

The following is an example of the password prompt dialog box. In the **User name** field, our name will be listed. Other names may be listed as well if there are multiple people using Lotus Notes on the PC. The **At location** field is where we select the location we are currently accessing Lotus Notes from. For example, we may be in the office or working remotely. If we have forgotten our password, we can expand the **Forgot your password** section as shown in the dialog box for instructions on what we need to do.

Closing Lotus Notes

To close Lotus Notes, select either **File | Exit** or click the red X in the top right-hand side. Be aware that one needn't close all the open window tabs before shutting down. For example, if we have our mail and calendar tabs open, we can leave these open; so, when we start Lotus Notes again, our e-mail and calendar tabs will be open ready for us. This option is controlled via a preference that is set by default; it can be turned off if one wishes. To turn off this preference, go to **File | Preferences | Windows and Themes** and uncheck the **On restart, reopen any tabs that were open when I closed the client** option.

When we close Lotus Notes and are in the middle of replying to an e-mail or creating a new calendar entry, Lotus Notes will prompt us to confirm if we want to send or save; so never fear, we won't lose any work!

Exploring the interface—where, what, and how

When we open Lotus Notes, we won't just see mail; there is the homepage that points us to important applications such as our Mail, Calendar, and even a Notebook. There is the Sidebar which, if enabled, is a valuable resource for interfacing with our calendar, RSS feeds, and Sametime contacts. There are many options to explore, so let's begin.

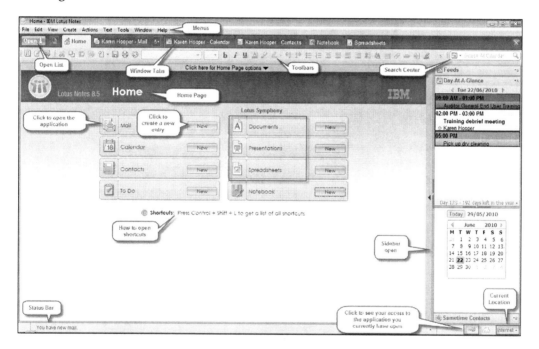

Window tabs

When we open an application in Windows, we will see it in the taskbar at the bottom of our computer screen (unless we have changed that option). When we open our e-mail or a message in Lotus Notes, a window tab appears for each opened item at the top, just under our menu options.

We can choose how we would like our window tabs to appear in Lotus Notes; these choices can be selected under **File | Preferences | Window and Themes**. The available choices are:

- **Open each document in its own window**: This option ensures that these windows appear in the taskbar of Windows—same behavior as Microsoft Outlook.

- **Open each document in its own tab**: This is the default setting in Lotus Notes.

- **Group documents from each application in a tab**: This is a great option if we want to keep our tabs more organized. The following is an example of this option. For the calendar, there are two pages open—**Mary Johnson - Calendar** and the **Weekly Management Meeting** calendar entry. If we select this option, the new way to close window tabs is the red **X** icon at the far right side of the window tab bar.

If we have selected to group our tabs, then we will have an option to close the group when we right-click on the tab.

 To close all currently opened window tabs, select **File | Close All**. An alternative way to close an opened window tab is to press the *Esc* button on the keyboard.

Window tabs can be rearranged by dragging them into a preferred position.

We can switch to a different window tab by pressing *Alt+W*. This will display a number for each window tab currently opened; type the number of the window tab we want to open.

Open List—better known as the button that says "Open"

As previously mentioned, Lotus Notes is more than just e-mail and calendar. A company can have several Lotus Notes applications that they use to track or store information. We might have created some applications of our own. So, how do we access these applications including mail, calendar, and so on? By clicking the **Open** button of course!

If we have Lotus Notes open, why don't we give it a try and click on the opened list? We should see icons with a title for each icon such as **Mail**, **Calendar**, or **Contacts**.

If we wish to open mail, we can select **Mail**. We will see **Mail** highlight as shown next; we can then click the left mouse button to open.

The Open list can be customized in the following ways:

- Right-click to select the **Dock the Open List** option. This will remove the Open List and instead show a bar called the Bookmark Bar positioned on the left-hand side of Lotus Notes with the icons but no title; we need to highlight each icon to see the title of the icon.

- Right-click to select the **Use Large Icons** option; this will change the size of the icons to large.

- If we wish to add a particular application, a message, or even stationary to our Open List, simply open the application or message and drag the window tab of the opened application or message to the Open List or the Bookmark Bar. This is similar to adding websites as Favorites in Internet Explorer. For example, to add the Notebook application to the Open List, open the **Notebook** application, click on the **Notebook** window tab as shown in the next screenshot, and then holding your left mouse button, drag to the Open List or Bookmark Bar.

- We can also search the Open List, by simply typing what we are looking for in the **Type to find** field just below the **Open** button.

Thumbnails

Thumbnails, when clicked, show a graphical presentation of what is currently open in Lotus Notes. A screen will open showing each window tab that is open. Thumbnails are located next to the **Open List** as shown in the next screenshot; the shortcut to open is *Ctrl+Shift+T*.

The following screenshot represents what thumbnails look like when opened:

Homepage

The **Home** page has links to open Mail, Calendar, Contacts, To Do, and the Notebook application. We may also see options to create new documents, presentations, and spreadsheets; these are available if we have Symphony installed (we will discuss Symphony in Chapter 11).

The following is a screenshot of the **Home** page:

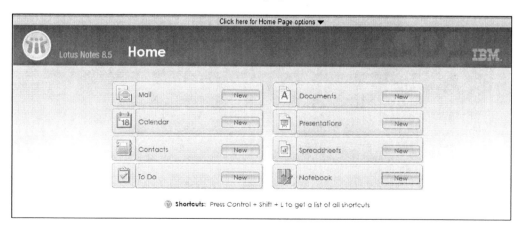

The **Home** page can be customized in a variety of ways. Select the option **Click here for Home Page options**, which is at the top of the **Home** page.

 A cool feature of the Home page is the Notebook application. The name describes exactly what it is — a place where one can enter notes. No one else has access to our Notebook, so the information we enter is private. On the **Home** page, click on **New** to create the Notebook. Once the Notebook is created, the **New** button will create a document where we can enter notes in the Notebook.

Shortcuts

On the Home page, you will see a shortcut to open a list of shortcuts!!!

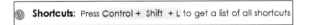

The next screenshot shows the shortcut list:

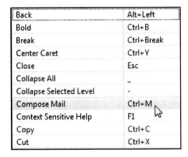

Back	Alt+Left
Bold	Ctrl+B
Break	Ctrl+Break
Center Caret	Ctrl+Y
Close	Esc
Collapse All	-
Collapse Selected Level	-
Compose Mail	Ctrl+M
Context Sensitive Help	F1
Copy	Ctrl+C
Cut	Ctrl+X

My favorite shortcut is *Ctrl+M* which, when selected, creates a message from anywhere within Lotus Notes. This comes very handy and quick as we don't always have to open our mail to create a message.

For a more extensive list of shortcuts, select **Help | Help Contents | Lotus Notes | Keyboard shortcuts**.

Toolbars

Toolbars are positioned under the window tabs and provide shortcuts to menu options. Toolbars within Lotus Notes can be repositioned, customized, and created. The following is an example of repositioning a toolbar:

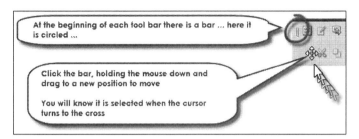

By default, many toolbars are context sensitive, which means they appear only when they are needed. For example, we see only the Editing Toolbar when we are typing text in a document. When we are in our Inbox, the Editing Toolbar is grayed out and not available to be selected. To see a list of available toolbars, right-click in the toolbar area. From this area we can select which toolbars we want to display in the toolbar area.

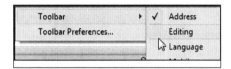

To customize a toolbar, right-click in the toolbar area and select **Toolbar Preferences**; from within here we can customize and create our own toolbars. Alternatively we can access toolbar preferences under **File | Preferences | Toolbar | Customize**.

Search toolbar

One toolbar which should be explored is the Search Toolbar. If we are in our mail and we want to search for a word within the subject, the body of the message, or the address fields, then simply type the word in the Search Toolbar and then select the *Enter* key or click the magnifying class icon. The search will occur on all documents in our Mail including our Inbox, Sent folder, Drafts, and personal folders.

We can also search our Calendar and Contacts and even do a Yahoo or Google Search. Each search that we perform is saved under **Recent Searches**.

To perform a search in our mail, type the words we are searching for in the **Search All Mail** toolbar. If we are in our Calendar, the search will be performed in the Calendar and so on. Once we have typed the word, click on the magnifying icon to start the search.

Alternatively we can click the icon in the Search Toolbar to show the drop-down menu. This option allows us to choose different places to search. In the example shown in the following screenshot, the search would be performed in **All Mail** as this is the option selected:

To perform the search, click the magnifying class icon or press the *Enter* key. A new window tab will open with the results of the search and it will also show all recent searches.

Search preferences

We can change the preferences available for searching. Go to **File | Preferences | Search**. In this area we can enable **Search History**, which is ON by default. There is also a button that we can select to clear history.

By default when we perform a web search, the results will be presented in the embedded browser in Lotus Notes. We can change this preference by deselecting **Use embedded browser to display Search Center web search results**. If this preference is not selected, the web search results will show in our default web browser.

We can change what is displayed in the search list. Go to **File | Preferences | Search | Search List**. We will see a list of what we are able to select; we can then check or uncheck the available options.

Finally, we can add our applications to the Search drop-down list. In the following screenshot, I have added **Karen's Training Resources** application to the Search drop-down list. To do this I opened the application, clicked the Search drop-down list in the Search toolbar, and then selected the option to **Always Show in Search List**. I can now, from anywhere in Lotus Notes, perform searches in the application by selecting the option in the Search toolbar.

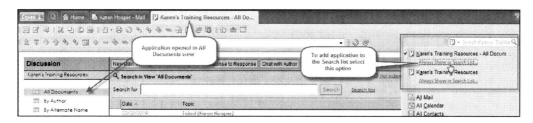

 One of the search options listed is Windows Search. This option searches our local drives and returns to the search view in Lotus Notes, links to the files it has found.

SideBar

The sidebar is located on the right-hand side of the Lotus Notes screen. It contains some of our key applications such as calendar, Sametime (which is IBM's chat application), and our RSS Feeds as well as Widgets and Activities. The concept of the sidebar is that one can be in his/her inbox working and see on his/her right-hand side what is on the calendar today in the Day-At-A-Glance panel of the sidebar.

What is available in our sidebar is determined by what has been made available in our organization. For example, our organization may not have enabled RSS Feeds; if this is the case, we will not see the Feeds panel in the sidebar. The following is a screenshot of the sidebar. This sidebar has three panels: **Feeds**, **Day-At-A-Glance**, and **Sametime Contacts**.

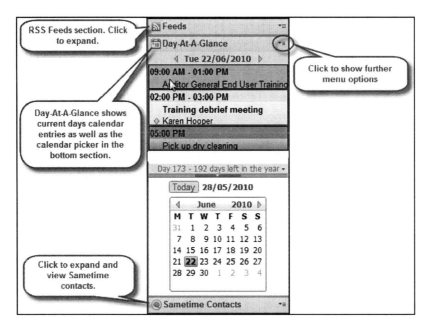

The sidebar has three states or three ways it can be viewed—open, closed, and thin.

- Open allows us to see all your sidebar options.
- Closed means it is not visible. We will have to click the small white arrow shown in the next screenshot to open.
- Thin means we see only available icons. We can click an icon to open the sidebar. The following screenshot shows the sidebar in the thin state:

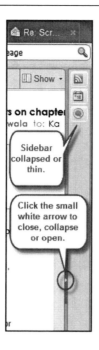

Our sidebar can have the following components:

- **Sametime Contacts**: Sametime is IBM's chat application. From within the sidebar, we have all the Sametime capabilities available to us such as seeing our contacts and, if they are available, being able to chat with current contacts and add or remove contacts, along with many other features. We may not see this option in the sidebar if Sametime has not been enabled in our organization. The next is a screenshot of what Sametime looks like in the sidebar. Sametime is discussed in detail in the next chapter.

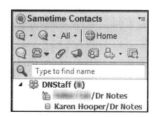

- **Day-At-A-Glance**: This shows the current days calendar entries such as meetings, appointments, and so on. We can use the arrows to go back or forward through the days or click in the calendar below to select a different day to view. If we double-click any of the calendar entries, it will open that entry. Alternatively we can right-click and select the **Open in New Window** option.

- **Feeds**: This shows RSS Feeds we have subscribed to. In this section, we can also manage and add new feeds. This is explained in detail in *Chapter 3, Feeds*.

- **Activities**: This application helps organize our documents under categories.

- **Quickr**: This is a document management application that integrates with Lotus Notes.

We can change which of these applications is displayed in our sidebar. Each of the panels includes a panel menu that we can use to manipulate the panel (including floating or removing the panel), as well as context commands for the application.

Lotus Notes browser

Within Lotus Notes, there is an inbuilt browser or embedded browser. The browser allows us to open and navigate web pages directly from within Lotus Notes.

We can change which web search engine the embedded browser uses in its search bar by clicking **File | Preferences | Search**, and then clicking a search engine in the list.

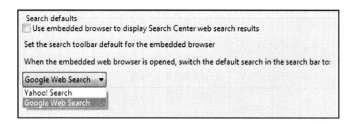

We can open the browser by:

- Clicking the **Open** button and then clicking **Web browser**. We can repeat this step if we want to have more than one browser page open.

- Typing a web address (URL) into the **Address** toolbar, and then clicking the **Go** button, which is to the left of the **Print** button. If the **Address** toolbar is not showing, right-click in the toolbar area and select **Address**. If we want to bookmark the page we have just opened, select **Create | Bookmark**.

From within the embedded browser toolbar, we can:

- Navigate to the previous page by clicking **Back**.

- Navigate to the next page by clicking **Forward**.

- Stop the web page from loading by clicking the **Stop** button.

- Reload the web page by clicking the **Refresh** button.

- Return to the page that is set as our Home page by clicking the **Go home** button.

- Print the web page that is displayed by clicking the **Print** button.

- Change the page settings for printing the displayed web page by selecting the down arrow next to the **Print** button and then clicking **Page Setup**.

- Preview how the displayed web page will look printed by selecting the down arrow next to the **Print** button and then clicking **Print Preview**.

The following is the browser toolbar:

Lotus Notes uses the embedded browser by default. We can disable it by accessing **File | Preferences**, clicking **Web Browser**, and then checking the **Use the browser I have set as the default for this operating system** option. This will mean that Lotus Notes will use Internet Explorer or Firefox for browsing.

Preferences

There are many options that we can select to personalize Lotus Notes. Some preferences may be set on one's behalf by the company's IT department as they have a set of policies that they can set that determines almost all of the possible preferences and features that might be available. For example, the IT department can set a policy for whether or not to show the Open List as a button, or whether to show it as docked.

We can customize Lotus Notes so that it operates and displays just the way we want it to. The following is an example of some of the available preferences:

- Basic settings that determine the look and feel of our Lotus Notes client
- Our Mail, Calendar, To Do, and Contacts applications
- Replication
- Lotus Sametime
- The IBM Lotus Symphony such as Spreadsheets (if available)
- Activities or Websphere Portal accounts (if an organization uses them)

We have already explored some of the preferences available such as window and themes and toolbar preferences.

To access preferences, select **File | Preferences**. There are numerous preferences that can be set; to simplify finding a particular preference, type the name in the field at the top of the preferences dialog box as shown in the following screenshot:

An excellent preference to enable is the **Document AutoSave**, which is available under the **Basic Notes Client Configuration** option.

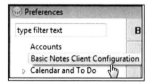

To enable, just check the box next to the **AutoSave every** field and then select the minutes. The default time is 15 minutes; in the following screenshot I have changed the time to **8 minutes**.

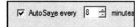

Once enabled, Lotus Notes can automatically save documents we are working on to prevent loss of data due to a system crash or power outage.

AutoSave is available within our mail file and any other databases that have been upgraded and the AutoSave options that have been enabled.

If a crash has occurred, on restarting Lotus Notes we are prompted to recover documents; if we select **Yes**, we will then be prompted with the following choices:

- **Recover**: This option will open the selected document and then close the dialog box.
- **Recover All**: This option will open all documents listed and close the dialog box.
- **Remove**: This option will remove the selected document from the AutoSave database.
- **Remove All**: This will remove all documents listed from the AutoSave.

There is a manual option to recover documents. If we choose to say **No** to the prompt received when we first open Lotus Notes after a crash, we can at any time select the option to recover documents by selecting **File | AutoSave | Recover AutoSaved Documents**.

Summary

In this chapter, we have explored the client interface of Lotus Notes, including the Open List, the Home Page, and the Sidebar as along with many other options. We should now be familiar with:

- Using the Open List and Thumbnails
- Features of the Home Page
- Available shortcuts (remember *Ctrl+M* creates a message)
- Use of the Sidebar
- Working with window tabs
- Toolbar options
- Preferences that assist you in customizing Lotus Notes to the way we want it

In the following chapters we will explore preferences further.

2
To Chat or Not to Chat: Lotus Sametime

With the advancement of technology and social networking, we can see certain forms of communication growing at a rapid rate, one of these being online chat, also known as instant messaging. There are various types of applications such as Yahoo Messenger, AOL Instant Messenger, Google Talk, and so on that enable us to chat with people far and near. Within Lotus Notes there is an inbuilt chat application called **Lotus Sametime**. For its employees to take advantage of the features of Sametime within the Lotus Notes client, an organization will need to install Sametime. This chapter will take the stance that your organization has installed Lotus Sametime.

There are many advantages that come with Sametime. First, it is relatively low cost; it is not like a cell phone call where one is charged by the minute. Another advantage is the ability to see who is available to chat, which is fantastic when we're communicating with people who are outside of their time zone or across the world, or even one floor down in their office building. Sametime is instant because we're online—people can start a chat with someone when they see them online and they can instantly respond.

Sametime is fantastic for corporations—both large and small. Many times we walk the corridors checking to see if someone is in their office. Now with Sametime we can see if they are online, offline, or unavailable; we can even have Sametime alert us when someone logs on or becomes available. Many corporations are encouraging their employees to work from home. This is where Sametime comes in handy—it allows us to communicate as though we were in the office and we can save our chats if important business decisions were discussed during a chat. It is also great for corporations that have branches or outlets in different regions. Being able to get quick responses to questions is important to businesses, and Sametime facilitates instant communication.

In this chapter we will learn:

- What is Sametime
- How to use Sametime
- Understanding availability status
- Adding Sametime contacts
- Chatting with contacts
- The chat window options
- Setting Sametime preferences
- Sametime help

What is Sametime

Sametime gives us the ability to chat or send an instant message to others in a secure manner. Have you ever sent an e-mail and then wondered when the person will be able to respond? Do you get too many e-mails? Does listening to voicemail drive you nuts? If your question to all these questions is yes, then Sametime is the answer. Sametime allows us to first check if the person is available online, this is called **presence awareness**. Then if the person is available, we can start a chat with that person to see if he/she responds. Many people might say, why not just give them a call? Well, without Sametime you can't tell if the person is available — they could be in a meeting or they could be on the phone, plus there may be a cost to the call. So, being able to chat with a person using Sametime will typically give us instant results. Some other great features of Sametime are:

- It allows us to chat with two or more people at the same time, referred to as **multi-way chat**.
- There is an out of the box integration supported with e-mail and productivity applications such as Microsoft Office, Microsoft Outlook, Microsoft SharePoint, and IBM Lotus Notes.
- It has the ability to add or show rich text, timestamps, perform a spell check, and use emoticons in a chat session.
- Sametime also has the ability to search for contacts and display their details.
- It saves chat history so that one has a record of the conversation if required.
- Sametime helps manage our contact list by being able to sort, show short names, or show online contacts only.

Sametime is included when we purchase Lotus Notes; however, some companies extend their license to include extra functionality. The following are the features of the standard and advanced versions, but be aware that there are more versions available. The license that is included with Lotus Notes is referred to as "Limited Use".

Standard version:

- Built-in VoIP and point-to-point video
- Ability to transfer files via Sametime, and create, capture, and send screenshots
- Location awareness that automatically determines whether one is working from home or the office, and others can see this in their business card
- Contact information that can show photos and details of contacts when we float over their name
- Managed interoperability with supported public IM networks such as AOL
- The ability to conduct web conferencing, allowing us to start online meetings and share presentations
- Integration with supported audio, video, and telephony systems

Advanced version:

- The ability to search for experts and answers, even when one doesn't know who to ask
- The ability to capture and reuse shared knowledge, reducing the burden on subject matter experts and on our help desk
- Provides a forum for teams to share information in real time
- Helps in fast communication by instantly sharing our screen with our coworkers for document review or clarifications

In a company, Sametime might only have the ability to see the online status of people (presence awareness) and the ability to chat. For others, they may be able to chat and conduct online meetings. If one has the advanced version, then he/she may be able to use Sametime in a much more feature-rich way. In this chapter, we will focus on presence awareness and chat capabilities. To learn more about the standard, advanced, and other versions of Sametime, please visit the Lotus website at `http://www.ibm.com/sametime`.

The following is what the Sametime panel looks like when opened in sidebar:

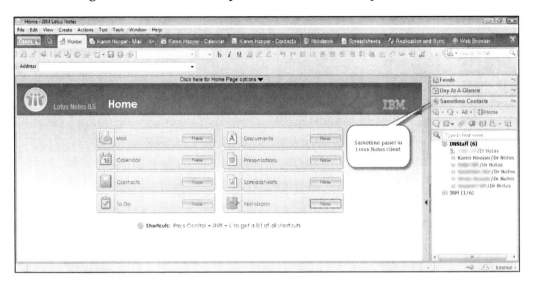

The Sametime panel has many options available that we will discuss throughout this chapter. To see menu options, click the menu icon to the right of **Sametime Contacts** as shown in the following screenshot. We can also view the menu by selecting **Tools | Sametime** from the Notes' client menu.

If we cannot see the Sametime panel in the sidebar, we also have the option to select **View | Right Sidebar Panels | Sametime Contacts**, and click **Sametime Contacts**.

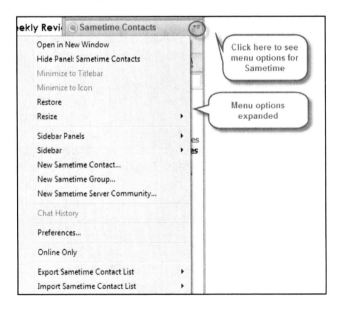

Many people like to leave the Day-At-A-Glance open in their sidebar, so that we can see our Sametime contacts' select the menu option and then **Open in New Window**. This will float the Sametime contacts for easy access.

How to use Sametime

We will now explore how to use Sametime including chatting, presence awareness, and setting preferences. However, before we can use Sametime, we must first log in by providing our username and password — this is part of the security that Sametime offers. This authenticates us with our organization and then chat transcripts are encrypted, which means no one else can read or access them.

There are two ways we can log in:

- Clicking the **Log In** option on the Sametime panel if available.

- Selecting the Sametime icon and then select **Log In** from the menu. When we log in, our current status will default to available; however, there are other status options available for us to select from.

Now that we are logged in, we will be able to see the availability of others.

Understanding availability status

Availability status icons appear next to people's names in Sametime, in our sidebar, inbox, contacts, and any Lotus Notes applications that have been Sametime enabled.

The following screenshot shows the Sametime contacts in the sidebar:

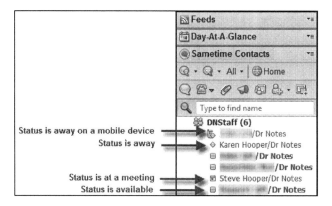

These icons indicate who is online, who are available to chat, and so on.

Others in our company can also see our current status, so the first thing we will look at is how to change our status. We will need to complete the following steps:

1. Click 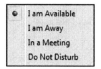 situated in the top left-hand corner of the Sametime sidebar panel.

2. Select status from the available choices; current selected status is **I am Available**.

3. Each status has a particular icon; the following table describes each icon:

Icon	Default icon name	Description
	I am Available	The person is online and available to chat.
	I am Away	The person is online, but away from his/her machine. When you send a chat to a person whose status is "I am Away," the chat is displayed for the person to view upon returning. (It is like leaving a Post-it note on their computer screen.)

Icon	Default icon name	Description
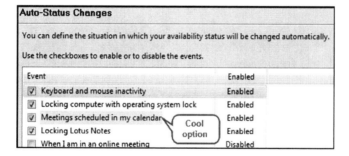	In a Meeting	The person is online, but in a meeting. This icon shows for all those who are not in the meeting. Participants in the meeting see this person as available.
	Do Not Disturb	The person is online, but does not want to be disturbed. If someone attempts to start a chat with us, they will be prompted that we have requested not to be disturbed and they will be given the option to e-mail us. We can set our status to Do Not Disturb while remaining available to specific individuals using privacy preferences.
No icon		The person is offline and unavailable.

We can set Sametime to change your status automatically, which is a good option, by completing the following steps:

1. Select **File | Preferences | Sametime | Auto-Status Changes.**

2. Check the situation in which we want our availability status to change.

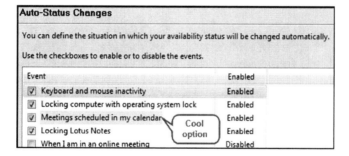

An excellent option is **Meetings scheduled in my calendar**; our status will automatically be changed when we are in meetings.

3. Next, select preferred choices for **Keyboard and mouse inactivity**.

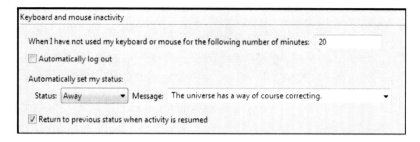

4. Click **Apply** and then **OK**.

Now that we know how to work with the different statuses, we should learn how to add contacts.

Adding Sametime contacts

We have now logged into Sametime, we've set our status, and we are available to chat, but we don't have anyone listed in our Sametime contacts, so let's work out how to add Sametime contacts. Note that we can add an individual or a group.

We can add an individual contact in various ways:

*   Right-click and select a person in mail, calendar, or contacts. Then right-click and select the person's name, which will be listed first in the menu, and then select the **Add to the Sametime Contact List...** option.

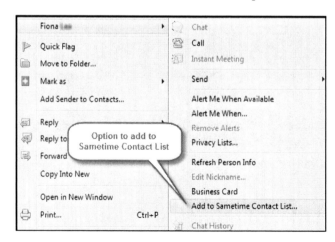

- Drag mail messages to the Sametime contact list. Select a message within the inbox from a person we want to add to our Sametime contacts and drag the message to our Sametime contact list; it will add the sender of the message to our contact list in Sametime.

- Click the **New** button in the Sametime chat window. If a colleague who is not listed in our Sametime contacts list starts a chat with us from within the chat window, select the icon to add that person to our Sametime contact list as shown in the next screenshot:

- Click the **New** button in the Sametime sidebar. From the Sametime contacts area in the sidebar, select the icon to add either an individual or group.

Chatting with contacts

We are now ready to chat, so how do we start a chat? There are several ways, which are explained here:

- Double-click the name of a contact to open a chat window with.

- Right-click a person in Sametime contact list and then select **Chat** from the menu.

- Alternatively, select a message in mail, right-click, and then select the person's name, which will be at the top of the right-click menu. We will then see another menu appear that has the **Chat** option at the very top.

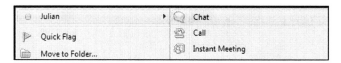

- We can also chat with someone not on our contact list. In the **Type to find name** field located at the top of the Sametime panel in the sidebar, type the contact's name and then press the *Enter* key. Now names that match our search will appear; select the contact we want to chat with and then press the *Enter* key again. If they are online, a chat window will appear, and if they are not online, it will give an option to send an e-mail.

- We can see the online status of people within our organization from within our e-mail, calendar, and our contacts. In our organization, we may also have some applications such as mail, calendar, and contacts that are Sametime enabled.

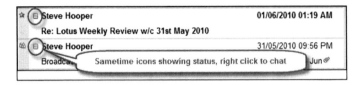

We can then select a person, right-click on his/her name, and select **Chat**.

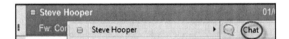

Multi-way chat

As we mentioned earlier, we can have multi-way chats that allow us to invite others into our current chat or select several contacts in Sametime and start a chat with them.

- Multi-way chat can be started by inviting others to join by clicking the **Invite Others...** icon as shown next. We can also accomplish this by going to the **Tools** menu and selecting **Invite Others**.

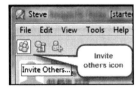

- To select more than one contact in multi-way chat, use the *Ctrl+left-click* option; then right-click and select the option **Chat**. This will open a new chat window that shows the number of current participants in the left-hand side. Each invited participant gets the option to either **Join the Chat** (to participate in the chat) or **Decline** (to close the invitation without joining the chat). The following is a screenshot of the invitation we will receive.

Once we have started a chat, we will see the chat window as shown in the following screenshot. Within the bottom frame of the chat window, we can enter our replies, add graphics, links, and emoticons. In the top frame, we can see the conversation of all involved in the chat. The following is an example of a two way chat.

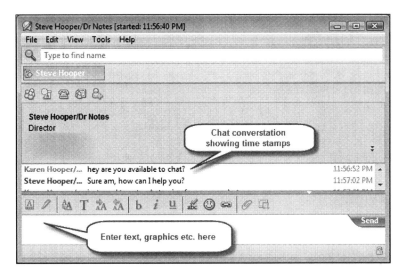

When we have finished chatting, we can close the chat window by selecting **File | Close** or click the **X** icon in the top right-most corner of the window. If we have specified where to save chat transcripts, the chat transcript is automatically saved when we leave. We can also set a preference to be prompted to save the chat when we close it.

Chat window options

There are several options that are available from within the chat window:

- We can change the color of your text foreground and background color.

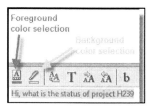

- We can return to the default font properties if changed, select different font options by selecting text properties, or increase or reduce font size.

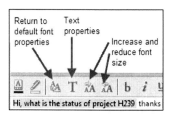

- In the chat window, we can run spell check and add emoticons and a hyperlink. We also have the ability to add attachments.

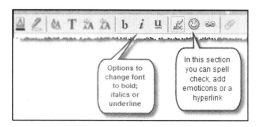

- The following is a screenshot of available emoticons. We can add to these by selecting the **Edit** button and then **Add Picture**. We can also add emoticons via **File | Preferences | Sametime | Emoticon Palettes**.

- There is also a facility to insert a hyperlink for a web address by clicking the chain link icon next to the emoticon icon.

A dialog box will appear when we select the hyperlink icon. We can either type the URL or paste it in by clicking the paste icon to the right of the **Link** field. In the following example, I have pasted a link to a Lotus Notes application. To create an application link, open the application we want to link to and then select **Edit | Copy As | Application Link**.

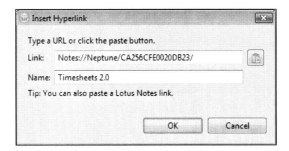

- When we type text in our chat window, we will see that misspelled words will be underlined with a red squiggly line as shown in the following screenshot. We can right-click to view suggested correct spellings or select the **Ignore All** or **Add to Dictionary** option.

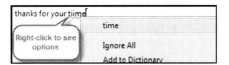

- There is also an option to print a chat transcript. To do this select **File | Print...** from the chat window.

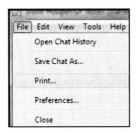

Setting Sametime preferences

There are many preferences that we can set so that Sametime is just how we like it! We have already seen how to set our preference for changing our status automatically. It is worth exploring the Sametime preferences available for us to be aware of all our options.

To access the Sametime preferences, select **File | Preferences | Sametime**.

The following is a screenshot of preferences for Sametime. Be aware that depending on a company's version of Sametime, not all the options will be available and so one will not be able to set preferences for them.

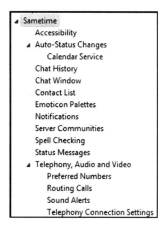

It is recommended to review all the preferences available. The following sections will highlight three of the available and most common preferences—**Chat History**, **Chat Window**, and **Notifications**.

Chat History

Within preferences, we can set how we want to save chat history. We will be able to select where we want to save chats - either in our Lotus Notes mail or in a local file. If we select not to save chats, we can always save a chat manually by selecting the **File | Save** option. The following is a screenshot of our default options for saving chats:

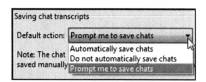

Chat Window preferences

There are several options available within preferences for the chat window.

The chat window preferences are in three sections—**Display settings**, **Typing area**, and **Set notification for new chats** (also listed in the main list of preferences).

The following is a screenshot of the available display settings; we can choose to select all of the available options or just ones relevant to us:

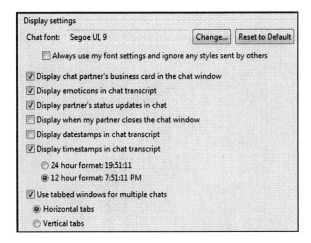

Tabbed windows tip:

The tabbed windows option is excellent for reducing the number of windows we have open on our computer as, at times, we may be chatting to multiple people. If you select the tabbed window option, Sametime will open only one window but each chat will be separated by a tab that can be shown vertically or horizontally. The following is a graphic where the preferences have been set to tab horizontally.

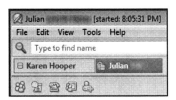

Under the **Typing area** option, we can select the direction of text:

The next set of options for the chat window are warning options, useful in situations such as when the person we want to chat with is away or in a meeting, and so on. We can also select how to close the chat window and what happens when we press the *Enter* key. We will review the **Set notification style for new chats** option in the next section.

Chat Notification preferences

People like to be notified of chats in different ways—for example, you may like the chat window to come to the front of your computer screen, others like the chat window to flash in the task bar, while a few may just want a sound to play. The following screenshot shows the options available for a new chat. Make sure we go into Sametime preferences to set up our preference by selecting **File | Preferences | Sametime | Notifications**. We can also access this area from **File | Preferences | Sametime | Chat Window** and then select **Set notification style for new chats** at the bottom of the dialog box.

In the **Event** area, we can see the different events for being notified and we can select each option. We can then select a sound and any other preferences that are available.

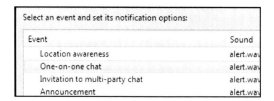

For example when we select the **One-on-one chat**, we can see the following options:

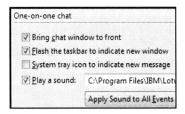

Sametime help

Sametime help is available from within a chat window as in the following screenshot, or alternatively we can select the **Help** menu in Lotus Notes and select Sametime from the available choices. Help will assist with providing further information about Sametime.

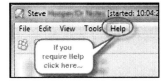

Summary

In this chapter, we have learned about the advantages of Sametime and how to use Sametime to chat and see the availability of people online. We discussed how to chat, add contacts, how to set chat preferences, and how to refer to help if we need further information.

In the next chapter, we will discover another tool available within Lotus Notes called Feeds. Feeds can assist with keeping you up-to-date with the latest information without clogging up your inbox.

3
Feeds

Have you ever subscribed to a website to get special bulletins, news headlines, or newsletters sent directly to your e-mail account? I have subscribed to quite a few but find that they tend to clutter up my inbox.

There is a new option for subscribing — web feeds. **Feeds** are a standardized web format used to publish frequently updated websites such as blog entries, news headlines, and so on. Feeds have many benefits over e-mail subscriptions, a major benefit being we do not have to provide personal information such as an e-mail address while subscribing. Feeds can be set up in Lotus Notes with ease, as we will see in the following pages.

More and more companies are enabling their websites with feeds. So, having a good understanding of the abilities of feeds will be helpful for us. In this chapter, we will delve into what a feed is and how to set them up in Lotus Notes. We will also look at how to view feeds. Then we will see how to set up our feeds so that we always receive the latest content from the websites we are interested in.

To summarize, this chapter will cover:

- What are feeds
- How to add feeds
- Viewing feeds
- How to manage our feeds

Adding feeds

A web feed is also known as RSS Feed. **RSS** stands for **Really Simple Syndication** and provides people with frequently updated content from websites. Content distributors syndicate a web feed, thereby allowing users to subscribe to it. Typically, feeds provide people with a summary of any recently added information or content such as a news headlines or blog entries to a website.

Most often there are several sites that we want to subscribe to and there are tools that allow us to subscribe to these websites and have those feeds come into one place. Such a tool or software is known as a **feed reader** or **aggregator**.

Many companies including news-related sites, blog sites, and many government and corporate sites distribute their content as web feeds. To know if a website is enabled for feed subscriptions, look for the feeds icon. The examples below can be placed anywhere on the website, however, typically we will see them placed somewhere on the first page.

Often we can select what we want to subscribe to—for example, if it is a blog website, then we may be able to subscribe to the content or the comments that people make; on the other hand, if it is a news website, then we can select if we want content on sports or business. When we enable our subscription, we select how often we want to be updated and how long we want to keep the information. We will look into this in more detail further on in the chapter.

Feeds sidebar panel

Feeds can be accessed and managed from within the Lotus Notes sidebar. We learned about the sidebar in *Chapter 1, First Impressions (The Client Interface)*. The following is a screenshot of the Lotus Notes client with the **Feeds** sidebar expanded:

If we can't see the **Feeds** sidebar panel, select **View | Right Sidebar Panel** and select **Feeds**. The **Feeds** panel can be collapsed by clicking click on **Feeds** in the sidebar. If we click on another panel in the sidebar such as the **Day-At-A-Glance**, then **Feeds** will close and we will see **Day-At-A-Glance** panel expanded in the sidebar. If we want to display our feeds separately, we can select **Open in New Window** when we right-click the **Feeds** option in the panel.

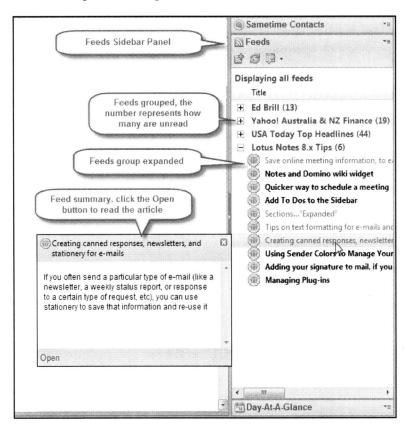

Indentifying feed-enabled websites

First, we need to identify if the website we are visiting has enabled syndication of its content (the fancy way of saying you can subscribe to it). We can tell if a website or blog syndicates its content by the feed icons displayed on the site, usually on the front page.

We may also see the feed icon in the navigation toolbar of our browser. The following is an example of a web blog by Ed Brill, who is the Director of Product Management at IBM Lotus Software:

The following is an example of a news website, USA Today:

Both of these websites allow us to subscribe using feeds.

Alternatively, on the USA Today website, we also see an area at the bottom of the front page that gives choices for subscriptions — the RSS option is circled in red.

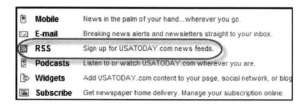

Once we have identified a website that is RSS enabled, there are a number of ways to add it to our Lotus Notes feed reader.

Adding feeds to Lotus Notes

Let's use the USA Today website as an example. There are a three different ways we can add feeds to Lotus Notes.

1. Click on the RSS icon which, in the case of USA Today, is available on the first page of their website.

2. Add the feed using any of the following techniques:

   ° Drag the RSS icon to the area where feeds are listed in our **Feeds** sidebar panel (make sure you hold your left mouse button down). This will open the **Add New Subscription** dialog box in Lotus Notes.

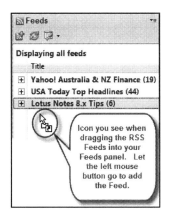

° Rather than dragging the RSS icon, this time click on it. This will take us to another web page. Select the URL on that web page and copy it to the clip board. Then go to Lotus Notes and select the **Subscribe to Feed** button in the **Feeds** sidebar panel. The **Add New Subscription** dialog box will now appear. Paste the URL into the space provided and then click the **Go** button.

3. We can select our preferred options from within the **Add New Subscription** dialog box such as:

° Which feeds we want to subscribe to if it's a multiple feed name—for example, the selected feed name in the following screenshot is **Top Headlines**, which I would change to **USA Today Top Headlines**.

° How often to check for updates.

° How long to keep entries.

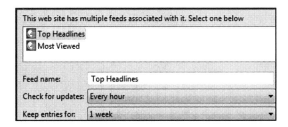

4. Once we have selected all our choices, click the **OK** button. This will close the **Add New Subscription** dialog box and add that feed to the **Feeds** sidebar panel.

Once we have added a subscription, we are given a choice as to how often we want the feeds to be updated and how long to keep entries for.

The choices available in the **Check for Updates** drop-down list are:

- **Every minute**
- **Every 10 or 30 minutes**
- **Every hour (default)**
- **Every 2, 4 or 8 hours**
- **Every day**
- **Once a week**
- **Manual (only check for updates manually)**

The choices for **Keep entries for** are:

- **1 day**
- **1 week (default)**
- **2 weeks**
- **1 month**
- **2 months**
- **Forever (only delete entries manually)**

Reading feeds

To read our feeds, we need to follow these instructions:

1. Make sure the feeds sidebar panel is open; if it is not, click on **Feeds** in the sidebar panel to expand.

2. Beside each feed name, we will see a + (plus) icon. Click on the + icon to expand and see the headlines. We will also see a number within brackets, representing the number of unread feeds. In the following screenshot, I have read all the **Lotus Notes 8.x Tips** and hence the number within brackets is **0**.

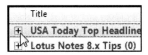

3. Click on a headline that we would like to read; in the following screenshot, I have selected **Swiss voters projected to ban new mosque minarets** from the USA Today Top Headlines feeds.

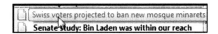

4. Once we click on the headline, a dialog box will appear with a short summary of the headline, with an **Open** button that we can click to open the headline on the website where it was derived.

Managing feeds

Once we have subscribed to some feeds, we may want to edit the feed subscription or we may want to unsubscribe. This can be achieved by right-clicking on the feed name or the headline and selecting one of the displayed options.

We can also select how the feeds should be displayed in the **Feeds** sidebar panel.

1. Click on the **Settings** button in the feeds sidebar panel.

2. We can select whether we wish to show all feeds or just one of the feeds. We also have the option to select whether we want to show feeds as a list, grouped, or managed fields. When we group feeds, it lists all the feeds under a heading and typically the heading is the website we are subscribing to. We need to expand the heading to see the feeds. Next to the heading title, we will be shown a number indicating how many feeds are unread, which is a handy feature. When we show our feeds as a list, the feeds are listed in date order.

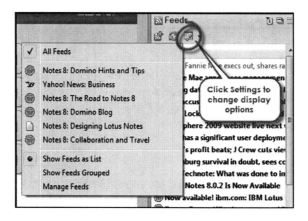

The **Manage Feeds** option allows us to select a particular feed and choose whether to unsubscribe, edit the subscription, refresh the feed which will show any new feeds that are available, delete offline content (if there is any), and **copy as link**, which creates a URL of the feed or headline that we can paste into an e-mail or a browser.

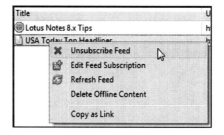

Summary

In this chapter, we gained an understanding of the usefulness and the value of feeds. When we do e-mail subscriptions, we obviously have to give our e-mail address. The benefit of subscribing to web feeds is that we can avoid giving our e-mail address or any other private details. Additionally, we can subscribe to numerous websites and have all the feeds come into the sidebar Feeds panel rather than into our inboxes.

We saw how easy it is to set up feeds in the Feeds sidebar panel, how to organize them, and most importantly, read them! In managing feeds we can determine how long we want to keep feeds. This means we don't have to worry about deleting them as they will delete automatically according to the timeframe we have set.

So now, rather than visiting all the different websites to remain updated, all the latest information on that website comes to us. Additionally, we can read and manage these feeds from the same client that we are accessing our mail, calendar, contacts, and applications from. Could this all have been any easier?

4

Working with Widgets

Some of you may know a widget as the small floating device that is found in a beer can, specifically Guinness! In Lotus Notes, a **widget** is a small application that you can install in the Lotus Notes sidebar. You can have several widgets installed. A widget can provide different types of information such as the weather in your area, stock prices on a day, and so on.

Widgets are great business tools as valuable information can be accessed quickly and can be customized to your preferences. You can also access some fun widgets such as comic strips, You Tube and even a virtual flower pot! Whether for fun or business, widgets are worth investigating. The topics we will explore in this chapter are:

- Widgets explained
- Adding widgets
- Live Text explained
- Setting up Live Text

Widgets do what!

To explain widgets further, let's look at some examples such as the LinkedIn widget from `http://www.linkedin.com/lotus` and Google Maps.

[LinkedIn is a business, social networking site that we usually access and manage via e-mail and a web browser.]

By using the LinkedIn widget, we can receive our LinkedIn e-mails and LinkedIn updates all in one place, which is the widget in the Lotus Notes sidebar. We will no longer need to have our inbox cluttered with LinkedIn e-mails and we don't need to log into the website either. Within this LinkedIn widget, we can search for people we want to contact and work with; we can also update and share our status. The following is an example widget panel in the Lotus Notes sidebar showing a LinkedIn profile:

Another widget that is very useful is the Google Maps widget. When used in conjunction with Live Text, it enables us to right-click on an address in an e-mail or a document and then locate the address on Google Maps, all within Lotus Notes. The following is an example of an address that is being recognized as Live Text:

```
120 E 87th Street
New York, 10128
```

Live Text, in conjunction with widgets, allows Lotus Notes to recognize and highlight specific patterns of text such as an address, an individual's name, or a currency value within an e-mail, calendar entry or document in a Lotus Notes application; it will depend on what widgets we have installed. Once we see the underlined text as in the screenshot previous, we can right-click to display a menu that will give us options such as looking up an address using the Google Maps widgets, searching for details on an individual using the LinkedIn widget, or converting between currencies as there are several currency converter widgets available to install.

Widgets, as mentioned, can be utilized as a business tools that provide information. The type of information provided depends on the widgets we have installed. We have already mentioned some examples of widgets such as LinkedIn and Google Maps; however, there are countless variations of widgets available with a variety of purposes and uses. The following is a sample list:

- World clocks
- Local and world weather
- Gas comparison
- Stock prices
- NBA playoffs
- Facebook
- FedEx/US track
- Dictionary and thesaurus
- Wikipedia search
- Zip code search
- Currency converter
- Learning plugin for IBM Lotus Notes

Our organization may have created their own widgets that allow us to access and work within some of our organization's Lotus Notes applications.

To add (install) a widget to our sidebar in Lotus Notes, we can select them from various places such as:

- A Widget catalog provided by our organization
- Google gadget from `http://www.linkedin.coters/gadgets/`
- Notes Widgets website: `http://www.noteswidgets.com/`
- Public widgets catalog at `http://greenhouse.lotus.com/plugins/plugincatalog.nsf`
- Other websites that have widgets or gadgets available
- Someone mailing us a widget

Widgets that we add to Lotus Notes will typically have a file extension of `.xml`.

Once we have a widget added to our sidebar, we can customize how that widget displays, which we will cover later in the chapter.

Widgets are where

If widgets have been enabled in Lotus Notes, then they can be found in the sidebar as shown in the next screenshot:

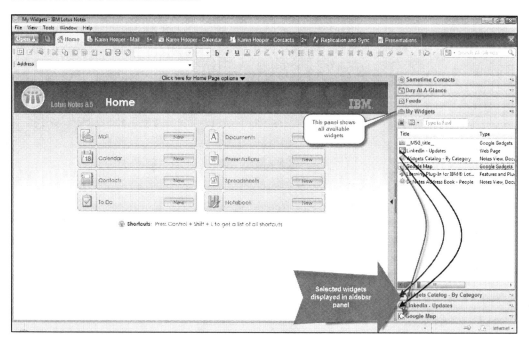

To be able to see widgets in the sidebar and toolbar, we have to enable them; go to **File | Preferences | Widgets** and select the **Show Widget Toolbar and My Widgets Sidebar panel** option. If our organization has a Widget Catalog server, (a Widget Catalog is an application that stores widgets. We can browse this application and select widgets we would like to add) we can enter the name or browse to search for the name. We need to ensure all necessary fields are filled in (note that the IT Department may have already filled this in on our behalf).

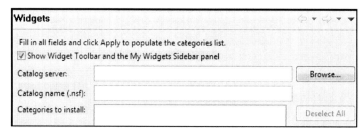

If widgets have been enabled within our organizations, depending on our IT Department's policies, we may or may not be able create our own widgets.

We can decide to hide the **My Widgets** panel in the sidebar if we prefer. Just go to **View | Right Sidebar Panels | My Widgets** and deselect the option. To show the panel again, follow the same steps and select **My Widgets**.

Adding widgets

As I have discussed, there are several places to select widgets from. I have given some examples of different types of widgets that we can add from different places. Following are the steps to add a widget from the Greenhouse catalog; from a web page and from the Google Gadget directory.

Adding a Gas Price widget from the IBM Greenhouse catalog

We will add a widget from the Greenhouse catalog, which is available on the IBM Lotus Greenhouse website: `http://greenhouse.lotus.com/catalog`. To use this website, we must register and give a business e-mail address.

1. Go to `http://greenhouse.lotus.com/catalog` (don't forget we will have to register with a business e-mail address) and search for gas prices as shown in the next screenshot. Click to open the **IBM local gas prices widget for Motortrend.com**. Once opened, click the **Start Download** button on the page and finally click **I Agree** on the license prompt page.

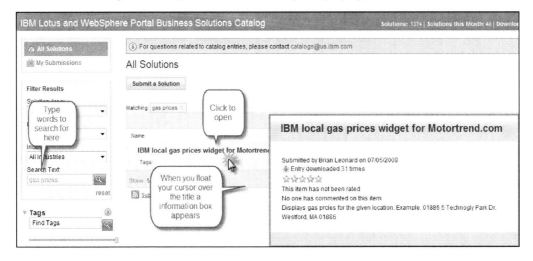

2. Once the download is complete, we will see a **Drag and drop install** area; we need to drag-and-drop this to the **My Widgets** panel in Lotus Notes. To make the drag-and-drop easier, I have minimized the browser and placed it beside the Lotus Notes sidebar. Make sure you have the **My Widgets** panel expanded before you drag and drop.

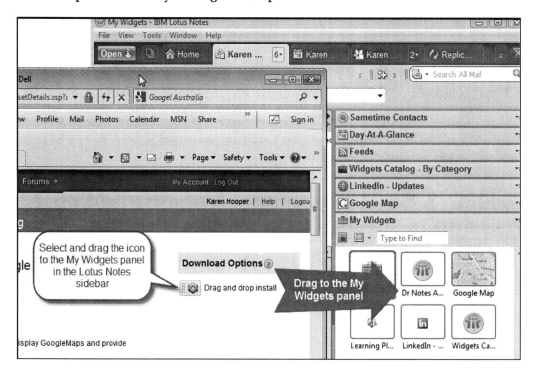

3. From within the **My Widgets** panel, right-click the newly added **Cheapest local gas prices** widget. Select **Open in | Sidebar Panel**.

4. Open the Cheapest local gas prices panel, add a ZIP code and any other criteria, and then click the **OK** button. Be aware that some widgets do not work in every country. You will to test each widget once added.

When we are running Notes client 8.5.1 and attempt to install a widget into the widget sidebar using drag-and-drop from the Greenhouse catalog, the Notes client creates the account in our preferences with no credentials and may give the following error: **Application failed using the supplied credentials. Verify the username and password and try again**. We will need to edit our account preferences using **File | Preferences | Accounts** and add our Greenhouse credentials in there.

Adding a Digg iPhone application from a web page

The Digg iPhone application is a seamless experience for browsing popular content from around the web and engaging in conversations around that content. The following are the steps to add the application as a widget.

1. In the toolbar, select the **Getting started with Widgets...** icon as shown in the following screenshot:

2. In the **Start Configuring Widgets** dialog box, select to create the widget from the second option which is **Web Page**, then select the **Next** button.

3. In the next section, select **Web Page by URL** and then enter the Digg website, which is `http://m.digg.com`. Click on the **Next** button.

4. In the next section, select the **This Web Page: Build a widget from this web page (HTTP GET)** option and then click the **Next** button.

5. A preview of the Digg application will be shown. Click **Next**.

6. Select the **Display as a sidebar panel** option and then click **Next**.

7. Finally click **Finish** and view the application in sidebar.

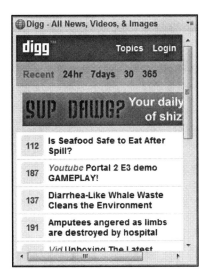

Adding a Currency Converter from the Google Gadget directory

The currency converter is a very useful widget to easily calculate currency conversions.

1. Open the **My Widgets** panel menu and select **Configure a Widget from... | A Google Gadget**.

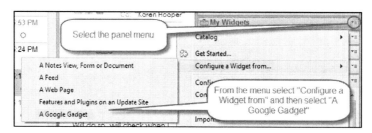

2. Select the **Browse the Google Gadget Directory** option and then click the **Finish** button.

3. In the browser window that opens in Lotus Notes, type **currency converter** in the bar and then click the **Search Google Gadgets** button.

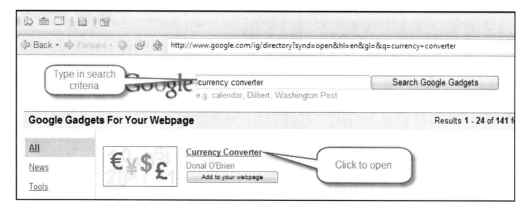

4. Once the results are displayed, click on **Currency Converter** to open the widget.

5. Click the toolbar icon **Add to sidebar** as shown next:

6. View the newly added gadget in the sidebar.

Widget options

When one right-clicks on a widget, he/she will see a menu of available options as shown in the following screenshot:

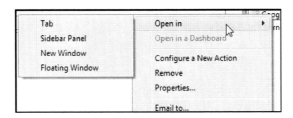

The following table shows a list of available options and their explanation:

Option	Description
Open in	This first option helps us decide how we want to display the widget. There are four possible options— in another **Tab**, in a **Sidebar Panel**, as **New Window**, or as **Floating Window**.
Configure a New Action	This option allows you to match an action with content from within an e-mail, calendar entry or Lotus Notes document.
Remove	This option helps remove a widget if we desire.
Properties	This option helps us review properties of the widget.
Email to...	This option will mail any widget in **My Widget** panel for the recipient to add it to their sidebar.

We can also use widgets in conjunction with Live Text.

Exploring Live Text

Live Text is text that has an action capability. It gives us various possibilities.

- It could be an address and the action may be that when we select an address we can open Google Maps to that address

- It could be a number and the action is that we can open a window to convert the number into another currency

- Finally, it could be the text of a flight number and the action available here could be that we can check the status of the flight

The following is an example of how Live Text appears; it is underlined and when we move our mouse over what is underlined, a down arrow icon appears along with pop-up text letting us know that we need to click on that icon for Live Text actions.

As per our example above, when we click the down arrow icon (**Click for Live Text Actions**) we can select to open Google Maps as per the following screenshot:

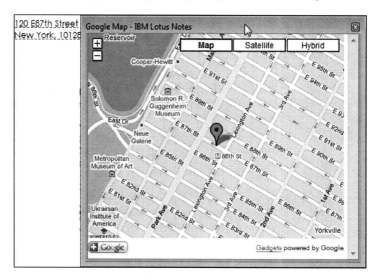

Live Text preferences

To ensure we can see Live Text follow the steps below. Our organization may have already enabled Live Text.

1. Select **File | Preferences | Live Text**.

2. Check **Enable Live Text by default for all opened documents**.

3. Choose the underline style.

4. The **Live Text Content Types** will depend on how Live Text has been implemented; in the example shown in the following screenshot, any addresses or cities will be underlined as Live Text.

5. Click **OK**.

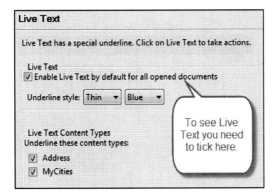

 Our organization may have selected to not implement Live Text. We may find that we cannot enable it in preferences, as these options would have been grayed out.

Summary

In this chapter, we explored Widgets and Live Text. We saw examples of some useful widgets that we can add. There are many other options and settings that can be configured for Widgets and Live Text. To explore further, check out the Help section in Lotus Notes; we'll find information under **Help | Help Contents | Lotus Notes | Widgets and Live Text**.

5

Mastering Lotus Notes Mail

Electronic mail is one of the most important forms of communications important forms of communication corporately as well as socially. Known by many names such as mail, e-mail, a memo, or a message, it is a convenient way of communicating, sending files, and reaching many people with one action.

Mail is a business tool that we typically use on a daily basis. When the mail system is down, many times work grinds to a halt! Because it is a tool that we count on, it is imperative that we understand all of its capabilities. It is like having a car that can save gas if we enable particular features; however, unless we know how to enable the gas saving features, we will get from destination A to destination B but won't be able to save gas!

This chapter helps us understand mail in more detail and will assist us with becoming more efficient in how we use Lotus Notes mail. Time saving features will be explored both in this chapter and the next chapter. In this chapter we will discuss the following topics:

- Accessing mail in Lotus Notes
- Creating and replying to messages
- Addressing messages
- Editing tools
- Attachments
- Viewing Mail
- Folders
- Mail icons
- Instant Spell checking
- Blank subject warning
- Signatures
- Deleting mail

Accessing mail in Lotus Notes

The first step in exploring mail is to open mail in Lotus Notes. There are a couple of ways that we can open mail:

- First, from the **Home** page by clicking the **Mail** icon as in the following screenshot. If we click the **New** button, it will create a new message.

- Also, by clicking **Open** and selecting **Mail** from the list.

Creating and replying to messages

In the following sections we will discuss how to create and reply to messages including reviewing message actions including setting delivery options.

Creating a message

Once we have opened mail, we can create a message by clicking on the **New** button and then selecting **Message** as shown next. As we can see from the message drop down list, there are other options available such as **Meeting**, **Contact**, and so on that we can create.

Another way to create a message is by using the keyboard shortcut *Ctrl+M*. This can be done from anywhere within Lotus Notes, not just when we have mail opened — for example, we can create a message when we are in our Calendar, from within Contacts, or from the Home page using the *Ctrl+M* option.

Message actions

Now that we have created a message, we will explore some of the message actions. Along the top of the message, we can see buttons that enable us to do certain things. The following is a screenshot of the available options. We will briefly explore each of these options.

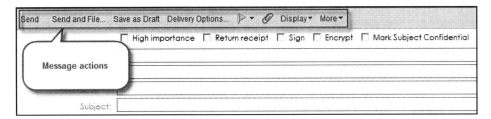

- **Send**: This speaks for itself; when clicked the message is sent!
- **Send and File...:** This is an excellent option when sending messages, as it allows us to not only send the message but also to file the message into our folders at the same time. When we click **Send and File...**, we will see the **Folders** dialog box with all our personal folders available. The following is a screenshot of the **Folders** dialog box that appears when we select the **Send and File** option. We would select the folder we want to file the message into and then click either the **OK** button or press the *Enter* key. The message will be filed in the folder; it will also be automatically filed into Sent and All Documents. Note that this does not mean we have three copies of the message filed in the three locations. There is only the one copy of the message in our personal folder; Sent and All Documents. This means if we delete the message from our personal folder, it will be deleted from the Sent and All Documents.

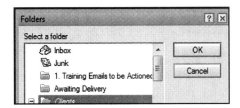

> When the **Folders** dialog box opens, if we know the name of the folder, we can start typing the folder name and that folder will be highlighted. Then if we press the *Enter* key, the message will be filed into that folder. Typically this is a quicker option than scrolling, especially if we have several folders. When you type the folder name you can see what you have typed in the Status bar, you can delete what you have typed if you have made a typing error.

- **Save as Draft**: This option saves our message into the Drafts folder.

- **Delivery Options**: Include options such as mood stamps and prevent copying (we will look at this separately in the next section).

- **Flag**: We can flag a message before sending it. We will explore flagging in more detail in the next chapter.

- **Attachment**: Clicking this icon will allow us to add an attachment to our message. Note that we can also drag an attachment into the body of the memo from Windows Explorer; we will go into more detail later in this chapter regarding this capability.

- **Display**: When we click on this button, we can see further options regarding how we want our messages to be displayed. We can select if we want to show the **BCC field, Additional Mail Options,** or **Sender Information**. The following is a screenshot of what we can see when we enable the **Additional Mail Options** option:

  - ° **High Importance** is indicated to the sender by a red exclamation mark.

  - ° **Return receipt** sends us a notification when the recipient/s have read or previewed the message.

  - ° **Sign** adds an electronic signature to the message to ensure it has not been tampered with.

  - ° **Encrypt** marks the message secret and can be read by only those whose name appears in the To, CC, and BCC fields.

  - ° **Mark Subject Confidential** prepends "Mark Subject Confidential" to the subject field.

- **More**: This is the last message action, from here we can access **Preferences...**, **Out of Office**..., and so on as shown in the screenshot. We will explore these actions in detail, later in this chapter as well as in the next chapter.

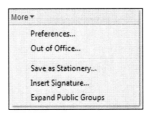

Delivery options

When we click the **Delivery Options** button in a new message, a dialog box opens with two tabs.

Basic tab:

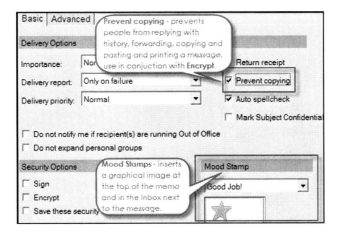

Note the difference between **Return receipt** and **Delivery report**—the **Return receipt** option sends us notification when the person has read or previewed the message, whereas the **Delivery Report** option tells us when the message failed to reach the recipient, which is the default option **Only on failure**. Other options available are **Confirm delivery** or **Trace entire path**; the later option shows us the server route taken to deliver the message.

Take the time to check out the **Mood Stamps**. I prefer adding the **Good Job** mood stamp to a message when I am congratulating someone. I often use the **Confident** mood stamp when I am sending a sensitive message. I will also select the **Encrypt** option that allows only those in the To, Cc, and Bcc fields to read it as well as **Prevent copying** which prevents people from forwarding, printing, copying to the clipboard and replying with history. Combining these options ensures the message is kept secure. The signing option adds digital signature to the message to confirm to the recipient the authenticity of the individual who has sent the mail.

Note that all three of these options typically work only for a message sent within our organization and may not be applied to messages sent to people external to us such as someone at another company.

Advanced tab:

On the **Advanced** tab, there are options that allow us to add a **Please reply by date.** We can also select that replies to the memo go to another person or several other people. We can also add our name. Some organizations have shared mail files such as Sales where messages sent to sales at the company name will go into a central mail file. It is preferable to add those addresses, along with my own, to the **Replies to this memo should be addressed to** field so that those we work with are kept in the loop with particular communications.

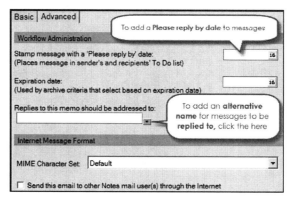

Replying to messages

We can reply to a message from our inbox or from within the memo. The reply options are:

- **Reply with History Only** (default) and **Reply to All with History Only**: This option includes the history of the original memo but does not include the attachment(s). Reply to all will include everyone in the To; CC and BCC fields, the reply option only includes those in the To field.
- **Reply with History & Attachments** or **Reply to All with History & Attachments:** This option includes the history of the original memo and the attachment(s).
- **Reply** and **Reply to All**: This option does not include any of the history of the original e-mails or attachments.

> When replying to messages, use the permanent pen function that adds our comments in a color that is different from the original message. We can also use the highlighter pen to highlight text in the original message for emphasis. Access the **Permanent Pen** and the **Highlight Pen** from within the Editing Toolbar.

Addressing messages

We can address a message by either selecting a recipient's name from our contacts or the Corporate Directory. We can also type names directly into the To, Cc, and Bcc fields. If we type names directly, Lotus Notes uses a type-ahead feature that completes names based on the first few letters we type.

How to address a message

It is as simple as typing a person's name but there are some other options available as follows:

1. When we create a message, our cursor will automatically go to the To field in the new message. If we know the person's name, we just need to type it and we will see a list of names appear. This list shows our most Recent Contacts as Lotus Notes keeps track of the people that we communicate with most often and moves those names to the top of our type-ahead list. Note that the list is not in alphabetical order.

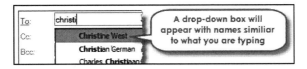

2. Many people have more than one e-mail address. If a person in our contacts has an alternative e-mail address, we would see an arrow as circled in the next screenshot. When we click on the arrow, it shows the alternative e-mail addresses as here:

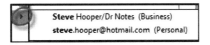

3. If the person we want to send the e-mail to doesn't appear in the list and we know that they exist in the Corporate Directory, click the option at the bottom of the list—**Search Directory for**. This option will show all the names in the Corporate Directory that start with whatever we have typed.

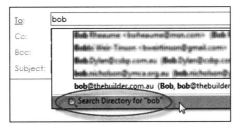

4. We can also select their name from our Contacts or the Corporate Directory by clicking **To**. This will open the Select Address dialog box and allow us to select the address book (directory) we want to search in (step 1). Type the name in the Find names starting with field (step 2). As the final step, add those people whom we have searched to the To, Cc, or Bcc fields by clicking the appropriate button (step 3).

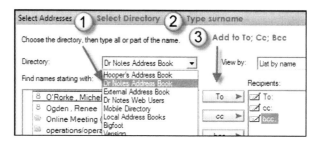

Protecting names in To, Cc, and Bcc fields

Often when we send a message, we are communicating with customers or suppliers, and there is a need to be discreet with what we allow to be seen in the To, and fields. We can utilize the Bcc field to allow only those people to see their own name. When the recipient receives the message, they will see only their name or Undisclosed recipient. Using this option allows privacy to be maintained.

 I use the Bcc field when I am sending e-mails to my son's basketball team as this keeps the team members' and parents' e-mail addresses private.

Prevent the expansion of personal groups

When sending a message, go to **Delivery Options**. Then on the **Basics** tab, check the **Do not expand personal groups** option. When the recipient receives the memo, they will see only the group name and not the individuals listed within the group. By default if this option is not selected, the group name will not be shown to the recipient, only the group members will be shown.

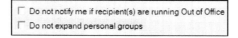

Formatting messages

Many times when we send a message, we want to format it in a particular way. There are several formatting options in Lotus Notes. Note that whatever formatting we can do in mail, we can also do in calendar entries, To Dos, and documents in Lotus Notes application which have rich text fields.

We can access formatting options in the following different ways:

- From the Toolbar
- From the Text menu as shown here:

- From Text properties, which can be accessed by the right-click menu or via the keyboard shortcut *Ctrl+K*
- From the right click menu there is a subset of formatting options available
- Using keyboard shortcuts such as *Ctrl+B* for bold

The following is a screenshot of the right-click menu, the formatting options are highlighted:

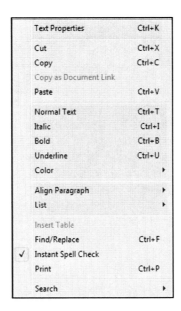

The Toolbar has several formatting options. The following is a legend of the Editing Toolbar for our reference:

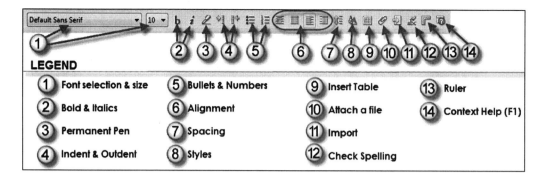

Here is an example of the text properties dialog box, which has several tabs with options. The following screenshot shows the Font **(a)** tab with the **Color** options selected:

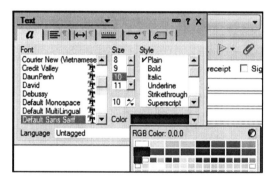

We mentioned as a tip the Permanent Pen and the Highlighter Pen as great tools to use when replying to messages because of their ability to allow us to show our text in a different color and also to highlight text. There is also the **Text Color** icon in the Toolbar; highlight text or put your cursor in a position where you want to change to another color then click this button to select a color.

Using the Permanent Pen and Highlighter Pen

To use the Permanent Pen, simply click the **Permanent Pen** icon in the Toolbar and start typing. To turn it off, we just need to click the icon again. When using the Permanent Pen, our cursor will have a pen-like icon.

To use the Highlight Pen, click the **Highlight Pen** icon and highlight text by dragging left to right over the text; to undo anything we have highlighted, drag right to left. To turn off the Highlighter Pen, click the **Highlighter Pen** icon again—basically it is toggle on and toggle off.

Changing the Permanent Pen font and color

By default, the permanent pen font is red, bold, and Default Sans Serif. To change these options, follow these steps:

1. Create a memo and put the cursor in the body of the memo.
2. Click on the **Text** menu, then **Text Properties**. Alternatively right-click and select **Text Properties** from the menu.
3. Click the Font **(a)** tab.
4. Select a font, size, style, and/or color.
5. Go to the **Text** menu and select **Permanent Pen - Set Permanent Pen**.
6. Discard the memo.

Dragging and dropping text

We can drag-and-drop text from within a document or message. We can also drag text from one document or message to another via the window tabs. We just need to highlight the text we want to move and then drag it to the desired location.

 Note: This facility is available with Windows® versions only.

Shortcut keys in Lotus Notes

The *Ctrl* key on our keyboard comes in quite handy when we are editing text within Lotus Notes. Following are some common usages of the *Ctrl* key within Lotus Notes:

Keyboard shortcuts	Description
Ctrl+B	Selected text is made bold
Ctrl+I	Selected text is made italics
Ctrl+U	Selected text is underlined
Ctrl+Z	Undo option
Ctrl+C	Selected text is copied
Ctrl+V	Selected text is pasted
Ctrl+X	Selected text is cut

Further formatting options

If we click on the **Create** menu, we can see more formatting options. We can add pictures, page breaks, a horizontal rule (which is similar to a thick line), sections that collapse text under a heading, computed text that allows you to add animated text, hotspots that can link to URLs or file links, tables, images, and objects.

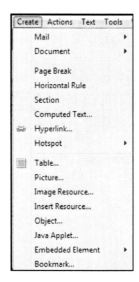

When copying an Excel® spreadsheet into a message, use the **Paste Special** and select **Paste link to source** from the options presented. This will paste the spreadsheet into the message. Now if we double-click on the spreadsheet, it will activate Excel®.

Note: If we add a table into a message or Lotus Notes document, we can copy the table and paste it into Excel® — the cells will be maintained and the information copied across.

Attachments

Many times, the reason we send a message to someone is because we want to send them a particular file. To send a file, we must attach it to the message.

Adding attachments to messages or documents

There are four ways to add an attachment to a message or document:

- Go to the menu and select **File | Attach**. A **Create Attachments** dialog box will open; browse here to select the attachment(s) we want to add and then click the **Create** button.

- Click the **Attach** icon in the Toolbar or the **Attach** button below the Toolbar. Both actions will result in the opening of the **Create Attachments** dialog box as it does when we select **File | Attach**.

- If we have Windows Explorer open, and our message or document is open in Lotus Notes, we can drag the attachment from Windows Explorer to the Lotus Notes icon in the Task bar, and then drop into the message or document we have open in Lotus Notes. If we resize the Windows Explorer dialog box to be smaller than the Lotus Notes window, we can simply drag from Windows Explorer straight to the message or document we have open in Lotus Notes.

The following is a screenshot of the **Create Attachments** dialog box; refer to the number legend to understand each area:

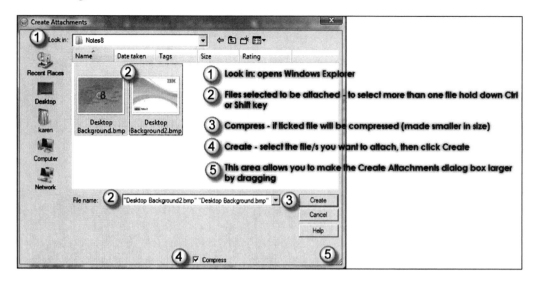

We can also drag attachments from a message or document to a new message or document. Select attachment, drag to tabs, go to new message or new document, and then continue to drag to the position where we want to place it in the attachment.

Working with attachments

Now that we know how to add attachments, we need to explore what we can do with attachments.

When we double-click on the attachment, we will see the **Open Attachment** dialog box as shown in the next screenshot. From here we can select **Open, Edit, View, Save**, and **Cancel**. Alternatively if we right-click, we will see more available options.

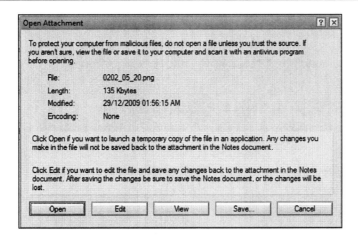

Opening attachments: Open button

When we click the **Open** button, the attachment will be opened in the program it was created in. For example, if it is a Word attachment, it will launch Microsoft Word and open the attachment. When we click the **Open** button, it is similar to when we are opening a Microsoft document in "Read Only" mode. Any edits to the document will not be saved unless we select **File | Save As.** Use this option only when we want to view the attachment in the program it was created in.

Editing attachments: Edit button

When we click the **Edit** button, it allows us to open and edit attachments. An example of where we would use this option is if someone has sent a message with an attachment that they require us to update. We would select **Reply with History & Attachments**, which creates a new message with the history and a copy of the original attachment. Select the attachment we need to update and double-click or right-click and **Edit**; the attachment will open in the program it was created in. Update the attachment and then select the save option in the program it was created in. The attachment in the message has now been updated and we can send the message. This is the only place where the attachment edit has been saved so make sure we save the memo by either sending it or saving it as a draft. If we need to access the edited attachment, it can be found in the Sent and All Documents.

Viewing attachments: View button

The view option allows us to open the attachment in Lotus Notes rather than launching the program it was created in. This option is excellent for viewing the attachment quickly; previewing zipped files without unzipping them; or for viewing files of programs we do not have installed.

Saving attachments: Save button

When we click the **Save** button, it opens Windows Explorer. We can browse to where we want to save the attachment(s) and then click **Save**.

Working with multiple attachments

If we have multiple attachments in a message or document, we can right-click one attachment and then select any of the available options from the right-click menu.

- **Save All**: This option will save all the attachments in the message to the location we select.

- **Save and Delete All**: This allows us to not only save to Windows Explorer but also to delete the attachments in the message, which will result in saving space in our mail. It will leave text indicating that you have deleted the file and give the file name deleted.

- **Delete All**: This deletes the attachments from the memo.

Printing attachments

We can print an attachment by selecting the **View** button, which will open the attachment in Lotus Notes (*not* in the application it was created in) and then select **Print** from the **File** menu or *Ctrl+P*.

Alternatively, to print the attachment in its original application, select the **Open** button and then select **Print** from the **File** menu, or use keyboard shortcut *Ctrl+P*.

Viewing mail

When we open our mail, we can choose to show our mail in different ways. For example we might select to show the preview pane or we might also want to show only unread memos. In this section we will explore these different options.

Preview pane

We can preview mail using the preview pane, which saves us from having to open and close each message. Previewing allows us to see the document's contents without having to open the actual document.

To access the preview pane options, click the **Show** button at the top of the inbox. From here we can preview mail on the bottom or from the side. To turn off the preview pane, select the **Hide Preview** option.

 I enable the preference **Mark documents as read when opened in the preview pane**, which is available in **Preferences** on the **Basics Notes Client Configuration** tab in the **Additional Options** area—it is the first choice in the list. As the preference name implies, when I click on an e-mail to preview it, the e-mail is marked as being read. I have selected this option as I predominately preview e-mails, so it assists me in keeping track of what I have read.

The preview pane is a separate frame that opens in the view or folder we are in, exposing a part of the document that is selected.

To resize the preview pane, select the bar that separates the two panes and drag to our preferred size.

 Caution: When we preview messages, a Return Receipt will be sent if it has been requested!

Conversations

We can view a message grouped with all of its replies so that we can read the message and replies at the same time. A message grouped with all of its replies is called a conversation and conversations save us the trouble of looking through our mail to find individual replies.

We can also act on all of the messages in a conversation at one time. For example, we could move all of the messages in a conversation to a folder by simply moving the conversation to the folder.

The following is an example of a conversation. In this conversation, there are two messages. The first message listed is the original, it is from Joanne, and the subject is **request for information**. Currently it is located in the inbox.

The second e-mail is the reply to Joanne from Karen Hooper that reads: **Thank you. Hope you enjoyed**. This was written in the body of the memo. This is because in conversations all replies listed show the first line of the reply, not the subject. This message is in the Sent folder.

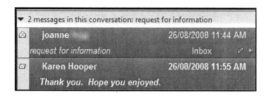

Viewing conversations

To view conversations, switch from **Individual Messages** (in which messages and replies are displayed and sorted individually) to **Conversations** (in which messages and their replies are grouped together). These options are available under the **Show** button—the same place you selected the preview options.

We can switch to conversations mode in our inbox, All Documents and our personal folders.

Once in conversations mode, the most recent reply in a conversation is displayed, and any other replies and the original message are collapsed below the most recent reply.

Following is an example of a conversation that has not been expanded; we can see that there are two messages in this conversation. We would click on the arrow head icon, which is called a Twistie, to expand or open the conversation:

When we expand the conversation, each message displays on one line. The original message displays its subject and each reply displays the first line of text in the body of the memo. When we expand the conversation the rest of our inbox is grayed out, to close the conversation click in an area in the inbox. The conversation will collapse and the inbox will no longer be grayed out.

We can stay in Conversation mode if we wish to. When a new message is received that belongs to a particular conversation, that message appears at the top or bottom of the inbox (depending on how we choose to show new messages). The message shows as being unread and the number of messages in the conversation is increased; we can also see who sent the reply, including the date and time.

 Note: Conversations can be viewed and sorted only by Date. Sorting by another column such as Sender automatically switches the view or folder back to individual mode.

The following table explains different actions one can perform with conversation.

Task	Description
Act on all messages in a collapsed conversation	Click the conversation to select it and then perform the action. For example, to delete all messages in a conversation, click the conversation and then right-click the conversation and select **Delete**.
Act on all messages in an expanded conversation	If all of the conversation's messages are not selected, click the conversation header to select all of the messages and then perform the action.
Act on one message in a conversation	If necessary, expand the conversation. Then click the message to select it, and perform the action. For example, to delete a message in a conversation, click the message to select it, then right-click the message and select **Delete**.

Deleting a conversation

When we delete a conversation, we will be prompted as shown in the following screenshot, confirming that the individual is aware of his/her actions of deleting all messages within that conversation.

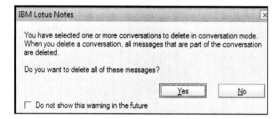

Turning off conversations

To turn off Conversation mode, simply go to the Show button and select Individual Messages. Or alternatively, when we are in Conversations mode, we will see at the top of the inbox, an information bar that tells us that we are seeing messages in conversation mode. To return to the original format of the inbox, click the **Clear** button; this will take us back to **Individual messages**.

Viewing unread mail

Often it is useful if we can show only our unread e-mails. To do this in Lotus Notes, we can go to the **Show** button and select **Unread Only**.

To return to showing both read and unread, go to the **Show** button and select **Unread Only**, or alternatively when you are viewing **Unread Only** you will see at the top of the inbox an information bar that tells you that you are seeing messages in unread messages. There is a **Clear** button that will also take you back to read and unread messages.

Once you have read a message you can mark it as being unread or select several messages and mark them as unread.

How to mark a message as Unread or Read

We can mark a message that is read as unread or vice versa by selecting the message(s) and then:

- Pressing the *Insert* key on your keyboard (it could be abbreviated as *INS*)
- Right-clicking and selecting **Mark as | Read** or **Mark as | Unread**

Managing mail with folders

All incoming mail goes directly to our inbox. After a while, our inbox can become quite large and one way to assist in managing the inbox as well as sorting our messages is to file them into folders.

Earlier in this chapter, we explored sending mail and the **Send and File** option, which allowed us to send a message and at the same time file it in its appropriate folder.

In this section, we will explore how to create folders as well as how to file received messages into folders.

First, let's start with how to create a folder.

Creating a folder

To create a folder, follow these steps:

1. Open mail and click the down arrow to the right of the **Folder** button at the top of the inbox.

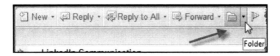

2. We will see the following options: **Move to Folders**, **Remove from Folder**, **Discover Folders**, and **Create Folder**—select the **Create Folder** option.

3. The **Create Folder** dialog box will be opened. The cursor will be placed in the **Folder Name** field; type the name of the new folder in this field. Note that folders are listed in our Mail alphabetically. If we want a particular folder to always be at the top of the list, we can prepend that folder with either numbers or letters. For example, to have the "Training" folder listed at the top of our folders, we can add either number "1" or letter "a" to the beginning of the name—1. Training or a.Training.

4. The next option is **Select a location for the new folder**. This option allows us to create a folder within another folder or to create a main folder. If we want this folder to be a subfolder of another, we can select the folder we want the new folder to be created in; if we do not select a folder, then the new folder will be the main folder.

5. Click the **OK** button to close the dialog box and create the folder.

 When creating folders, we can resize the **Create Folder** dialog box by dragging the bottom right-hand corner of the dialog box. This allows us to see our current folders and minimizes scrolling.

We may have noticed that when we have unread messages in our inbox, the **Inbox** name is bold and the number of unread messages appears to the right as shown in the next screenshot:

Folders are the same. When there are unread messages in a folder, the name of the folder is bold and the number of unread shows to the right; as the following example shows there is one unread message in the Int Dealers folder:

There are times when we create a folder and we need to rename the folder or remove it as it is no longer required. The following sections cover instructions on how to perform both tasks.

Renaming and removing folders

Often we create a folder, and further down the track, we may need to change the name of the folder or in some cases delete it. The following is how we can perform these tasks:

1. Expand **Folders** by clicking on the + icon next to **Folders**.

2. Select the folder to rename or remove, and right-click.

3. A menu will appear as shown in the following screenshot. Select **Rename Folder...** to rename the folder. We will then be prompted for the new name; enter the new name and then click the **OK** button.

4. To remove the folder, select **Remove Folder** from the menu. We will be prompted with a notification saying **this action cannot be undone, do you want to proceed?** Select the **Yes** button to proceed or **No** to cancel removing the folder.

We can also move a folder from one subfolder to another folder, or from a main folder to a subfolder, by simply dragging and dropping the folder to its new position.

Selecting messages

Often when we are managing our mail, we want to select several messages so that we can file, delete, or forward the selected messages to another person.

Selecting one or more messages or documents

We will often need to select documents so that we can file them, delete them, or forward them on to another person. The following are possible scenarios:

- **One or more consecutive documents**: Click a document, then press and hold the *Shift* key, and then click the final document we want to select.

- **One or more non-consecutive documents**: Press and hold the *Ctrl* key, and then click each document.

- **All of the documents in a view**: Click **Edit | Select All**, or **Edit | Deselect All**, or *Ctrl+A*.

- **Tick in left-hand margin**: There is a preference that we can select: **File | Preferences | Basic Notes Client Configuration | Additional options | Show check marks in margin for selected documents**. This preference allows us to click in the margin. We can also press the spacebar to select documents and use up and down arrow keys to navigate to different documents.

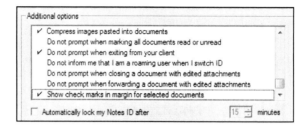

 Once we have a message selected in mail, we can perform the following operations: delete, print, archive, copy, forward, or mark as unread/read.

Filing messages

As we have discussed, folders are useful for organizing messages. We can put a message in one folder or multiple folders. When we select a message or several messages and then the **Move to Folder** option, we will see a choice to either **Move, Add**, or **Cancel**.

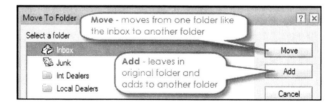

- When we **Move** a message to a folder, Lotus Notes removes the message from its current folder and puts it in the target folder.

- When we **Add** a message to a folder, Lotus Notes keeps the message in its current folder and adds the message to the target folder.

- When we select **Cancel**, the dialog box is closed and the messages are not moved.

When filing messages, if we use the **Move to Folder** option, the **Move to Folder** dialog box opens. If we know the name of the folder, we can start typing the folder name and that folder will be selected and highlighted. Then if we press the *Enter* key, the message will be filed into that folder. Typically this is a quicker option than scrolling, especially if we have several folders.

Caution: There is only one message. If we delete a message that is in multiple folders or views, the message is deleted from all of the folders and views.

The other way to file messages is to drag-and-drop. We can drag messages from our inbox and then drop them into a folder. To move a message to a folder, display the target folder in the navigation pane, and then drag the message or selected messages into the folder.

So now that we have learned how to create folders and file our messages, hopefully our inbox is looking more organized. In the next section we will learn how to find messages.

Finding filed messages

Sometimes we may file a message and then not remember which folder we filed it in. Other times, we may not have filed the message or we may be searching for a message that we sent. The next section discusses All Documents, which is a great place to find messages.

All Documents

All Documents contains all messages that are in **Inbox**, **Sent**, and our folders. In fact it shows every message in our mail, excluding deleted messages and is the perfect place to search for e-mails. If I can't find an e-mail in my inbox, I typically will go to **All Documents**, sort by sender, and look for the message there. To sort by sender, click on the column title. Basically all column titles are sortable; click once to put into ascending order and then click again to return to default sorting.

We can access **All Documents** in the side navigator under **Follow Up** as shown here:

In **All Documents**, there is a column that shows which folder the message is filed in. In the following screenshot, the **Folder** column is circled in red:

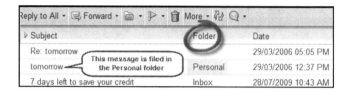

 Note: If we have the side preview pane opened, we may not see the **Folder** column or any columns. This is because there is not enough space to display the columns. In the next section we will learn what we will see instead is a **Sort by** button at the top of the messages where the column name would be. We can access the different columns by clicking the **Sort by** button and a menu will appear with the different sorting options as shown here, note the Folder column is not available from this area.

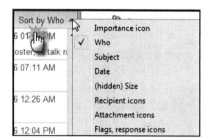

Discover Folders tool

Another way to find where we have filed a message is to use the Discover Folders tool. The following are the instructions on how to use this tool:

1. Select the message about whose folder location we want to know.
2. In the action bar, click **Folder** icon, and then select **Discover Folders**.

3. A dialog box will appear if the message resides in a folder and it will show the name of the folder. If it is in our Inbox or Sent folder, we have the **Add to Folder** option if we desire.

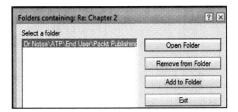

4. To close the **Discover Folders** dialog box, click the **Exit** button.

Mail icons

The following is a list of icons that we will see throughout our folders and views in mail. There are other icons but these typically are to do with Calendar and To Dos, and will be covered in later chapters.

Icon	Icon Help	Inbox Position	Description
☆	Unread Message	Left of message	Unread Message received, unread messages are bold or via preferences under **Fonts and Colors** can be selected to be **Plain red text**.
!	High Priority	Left of message	High Priority — when this person sent the message they selected the delivery option of High importance. ☑ High importance
↩	Message replied to Icon	Right of message	The green arrow represents the message has been replied to. If we open the message, we will see a History section.
↪	Message forwarded Icon	Right of message	The blue arrow represents the message has been forwarded. If we open the message, we will see a History section.

Icon	Icon Help	Inbox Position	Description
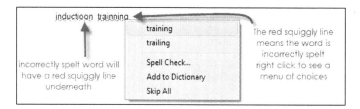	Message replied to and forwarded Icon	Right of message	The green and blue arrow represent the message has been replied to and forwarded. If we open the message, we will see a History section.
	Paperclip Icon	Right of message	The paperclip icon represents that this message has an attachment.

Spell check

When we are typing a message and we spell a word incorrectly, we will see a red squiggly line underneath the word in question. If we right-click on the word, we will see alternative suggestions for spelling as well as options to add the word to the dictionary or skip.

When we send a memo, if there is a word that is spelt incorrectly, we will again be prompted to correct the spelling. There is a **Send As Is** button if we want to bypass performing a spell check.

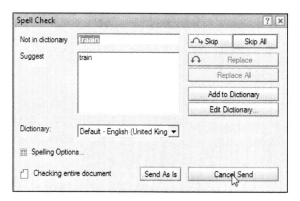

There are some excellent options to select in **Preferences** for spelling checks. I have found that people who work in manufacturing, or those who deal with part numbers, benefit from selecting the **Ignore words containing numbers** option as many of the part numbers that they deal with include numbers and letters.

The **Enable Instant Spell checking** option shows us instantly what we have spelled incorrectly by putting a red squiggly line underneath the word.

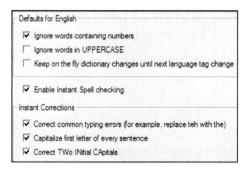

The **Instant Corrections** options speak for themselves and I have enabled them all as they are fantastic options.

Note: Dictionaries are provided for each country, so we need to make sure that we have selected our county's dictionary in the **Spell Check** preferences.

If we have set up our signatures, we shouldn't forget to **Add to Dictionary** our name and other details that are in our signature.

Subject warning

When sending a message, if we have not entered a subject, we are prompted to enter a subject when we attempt to send the message. When prompted, we can enter a subject and resend by selecting **Yes**. Alternatively, we can select **No** to send the message without a subject.

Adding a signature to messages

In Lotus Notes, as with other mail products, we can set up a signature that identifies us and our details. We can add our company logo, phone details, vCards, and even a web address. I have added my company title to my signature as well as my relevant details. To set up our signature, we need to follow these instructions:

1. Open Mail and click on the **More** button in the action bar at the top of messages. Then select **Preferences…**.

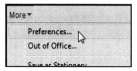

2. Select the **Signature** tab. Check the **Automatically append a signature to the bottom of my outgoing mail messages** option if we required. If we don't select this option, we will need to manually add our signature to messages by the **More** button in the message and selecting **Insert Signature**.

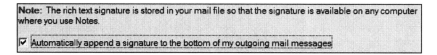

3. Click the **Append my vCard** button if we want to add a vCard attachment as part of our signature.

4. We can then enter then our signature and format it by clicking on the **T** then **Text**. We can also add graphics, paste in an image, or import an image, among other things.

The choices available under the **T** are as shown in the following screenshot:

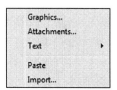

I have selected the **Automatically append a signature to the bottom of my outgoing mail messages** option. If I am sending a message to someone and I don't want my signature appended, I can simply highlight the signature and delete it from within the memo.

Deleting messages and restoring from Trash

Deleting messages is very simple within Lotus Notes. We can right-click and select **Delete** from the menu. We can also select the message and press the *Delete* key. We can also click the **Delete** icon in the action bar at the top of our messages, as follows:

When a message(s) is deleted it is immediately removed and placed into Trash until due to expire. We can restore deleted messages by opening **Trash**, selecting the messages we want to restore and then selecting the **Restore** button. We will need to restore before the message is due to expire, to confirm when Trash will be deleted go to **Preferences | Mail** and view **Delete documents in my Trash folder after # hours**.

Summary

In this chapter we have explored many aspects of mail in Lotus Notes. We have learned about creating, replying, and addressing messages. We also looked at the different ways we can edit messages. We explored working with attachments, folders, spell checking, and setting up signatures.

In the next chapter, we will delve into mail tools, which can assist us in being more efficient with the way we work with mail.

6
Lotus Notes Mail Tools

In the previous chapter, we navigated the basics of Lotus Notes mail. In this chapter, we will focus on the advanced features available and how we can best utilize them to assist us in being efficient with mail management.

Take the time to explore the available tools and you might be surprised to find that once we start using some of them, we might wonder how we ever lived without them. One of my favorite tools is **Stationery** — this is like a template for e-mails that I send on a regular basis such as a monthly report. Many colleagues I know have Stationery, which they have set up to send to their travel agent; it includes all their relative details such as frequent flyer numbers, passport details, and so on.

Another tool is **Copy Into New ... Memo/Calendar/To Do**, which copies the text from a selected message into a new memo, calendar entry, or To Do. I use this to copy details within a memo into a calendar entry so that I have all the details of the information in the memo right there in the calendar, which means I needn't search for the original e-mail.

I also love the **Find Available Time** tool, which is a context menu option available on messages, calendar entries, and To Dos. You select a message, for example of someone that you would like to meet with, and as the name suggests, it automatically finds the first time we are both available and gives us the option to create a meeting invite. It is a few less steps than doing it from scratch in our calendar.

In this chapter, we will explore the following topics:

- Senders Colors and Recipient Icons
- Collaboration history
- Finding available time
- Copying into Tool … Memo/Calendar/To Do
- Follow up Feature (flagging)
- Stationery
- Message recall
- Spell check

- Out of Office
- Managing Junk mail
- Rules
- Mail size indicators
- Archiving
- Mail Preferences

Senders' Colors and Recipient Icons

Often it is important for us to identify particular e-mails in our inbox quickly, specifically if they are sent only to us or we have been CCed, or if an e-mail has been received from a certain person. We can specify text and background colors to identify messages from particular senders. For example, we could use one color combination to identify co-workers on an important project, another color combination for our manager, and some other combination for personal messages from friends. We can specify several color combinations. In the following screenshot, background colors of red and blue have been selected for specific individuals:

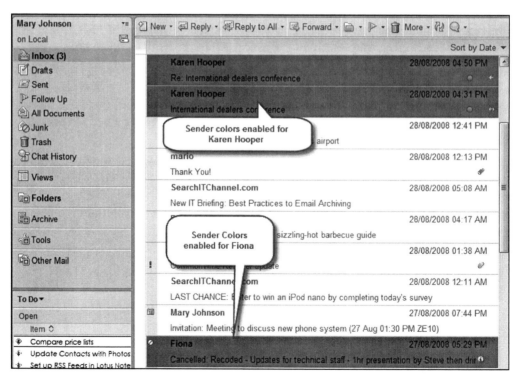

We can also display icons that identify messages in which we are the only recipient in the **To** field or our name appears only in the **Cc** field.

Specifying colors that identify senders

We can follow the instructions given next to enable **Sender Colors**:

1. If necessary, open your e-mail.

2. Click the **More** button above the message list, and then click **Preferences**.

3. Select the **Sender Colors** tab.

4. In the first **Sender names** field, enter one or more names of people whose messages we want to display in the first color combination. Separate names by pressing *Enter* (rather than using a comma as a separator). To select names from a directory, click the down arrow next to the field.

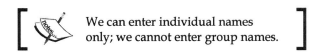
We can enter individual names only; we cannot enter group names.

5. Select a background color and or text color.

6. Click **OK**.

7. To remove all color combinations, return to the **Senders Colors** tab in **Preferences**, click **Restore Default Colors**, and then click **OK**.

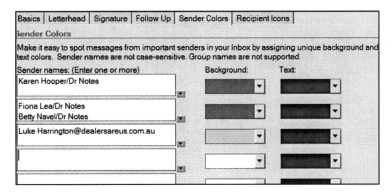

Displaying icons that identify your recipient level

To Cc a person in a message typically means that the message content is for information and we may not need to respond or action anything. E-mail etiquette dictates that if we want a person to take action on an item we have included in the e-mail, we add their name into the **To** field. It is therefore handy for us to immediately identify an e-mail where we have been CCed or an e-mail where our name is in the **To** field. The following are the instructions on how to enable this feature:

1. If necessary, open mail.

2. Click the **More** button above the message list, and then click **Preferences**.

3. Go to the **Recipient Icons** tab.

4. Select one or more of the display fields to display solid-circle if **Mail sent to me only**, half-circle if **Mail sent to no more than this number of recipients in the To** field and then select the number, or empty-circle icons if **Mail sent to me as a cc**.

5. To display the selected icons when mail is addressed to us with an alternate e-mail address or group name, specify one or more alternate addresses or group names in the field below, this step is optional.

6. Click **OK** to save the settings.

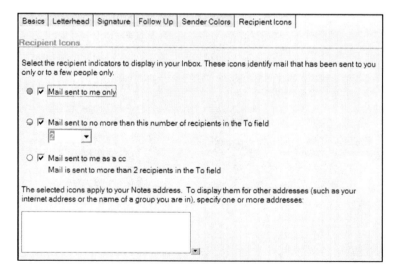

Collaboration history

Collaboration history incorporates quite a few features. We can view a history of collaborations or communications that we have had with one of our contacts such as e-mail, Sametime chat transcripts (if you have saved them), or meetings. Collaboration history includes all activity with a selected contact for the previous two weeks.

Viewing collaboration history for a person

Follow the instructions given next to see the options available with collaboration history:

1. From within your mail select a message from a person who you want to view collaboration history.

2. Right-click on the message and we will see the person's name that we have selected at the top of the menu options. This is marked as step 1 in the following screenshot.

3. Select the person's name and then we will see an extended menu. We will see an extended menu.

4. Select **Collaboration History**. This is step 2 in the following screenshot.

5. A dialog box will appear with a collaboration list; select and double-click to open one of the collaborations.

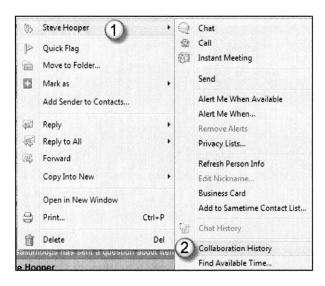

Finding available time

Often when we receive a message from a person and we realize that we need to organize a meeting with them. The **Find Available Time** feature is a great shortcut to show us the first available time for ourselves and the sender of the message so that we can create a meeting with them.

1. We can select the context menu by right-clicking on a person's name in our mail; we can then see their name listed at the top of the context menu.

2. When we select their name, an extended context menu appears.

3. Select **Find Available Time** to open the Calendar Scheduler and see when is the first available time for ourself and the person we have selected. If the person we have selected is an external person to our organization, the scheduler shows grayed out time slots as the information is not available; however, it does show our first available time.

4. From the **Calendar Scheduler** window, we can create a meeting as shown in the following screenshot:

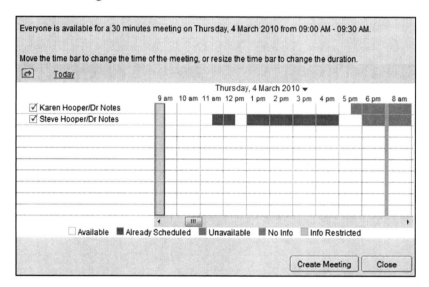

Copy Into Tool

Often we might receive an e-mail giving details that we need to paste into a meeting, memo or To Do. The **Copy Into Tool** allows us to select a **Message, Calendar Entry,** or **To Do** and then copy the information from either one of these documents into a new **Message, Calendar Entry,** or **To Do**. This saves us from having to copy and paste information between the message and the target document.

This feature is available from the right-click menu and under the **More** button as shown next:

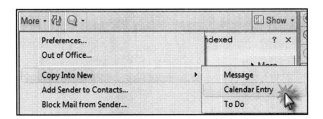

 One can drag a message to the **Day-At-A-Glance** time slots area to create a calendar entry from that message.

Follow Up feature

The "Follow Up" feature, or "flagging" as it is known in some other mail applications, is a fantastic tool for managing our mail. Many times when we receive an e-mail that we can't respond to there and then, we typically leave it in our inbox so that we remember to get back to it; we might even mark it as unread to further prompt us. The problem is that our inbox is designed for incoming e-mails, so as new mails keep pouring in our inbox, the e-mail that we need to follow up gets pushed further down the list.

Marking an e-mail for follow up assists us in managing those e-mails that we need to respond to, as it flags the message with an icon so it stands out from the other messages; we can also set alarms and view the flagged messages in a special follow up views to make managing them easier.

Flagging messages for follow up

Flagging messages is a great idea. We just need to select one or more messages in a folder or view and add a flag by performing any one of the following steps:

- Click the flag icon above the message list, select **Add or Edit Flag...**.

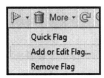

Enter flag priority, and follow up action, date, time, and alarm if required.

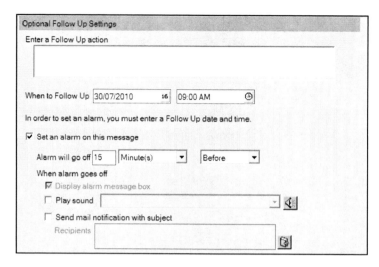

- Select a message or several messages and then drag to the **Follow Up** folder (this will move the message out of the **Inbox**). Then enter preferred options.

- Right-click and select **Quick Flag** (this will apply options that have been set in Mail Preferences).

The **Quick Flag** option is like a shortcut to flagging messages. Before we learn about the **Quick Flag** option, let's look at the several options that can be selected when we select the option to **Add or Edit Flag**.

 When we create an e-mail, we have the option to add a flag. This is handy when we want to mark an e-mail we are sending for follow up and it saves us from having to go to our Sent folder to perform the task after we have sent the message.

When we add or edit a flag, we will see an array of choices as to how we want to manage the flag depending on the importance and how we want to be notified. I will often use this area as a place to leave notes and set alarms for those messages that need more detail. If we have already added a flag and we want to change some of the options, we can select the same menu that we use to add a flag—**Add or Edit Flag**.

Importance

The first option we have is to select the flag priority icon that will be displayed next to the message or messages we have selected for follow up. There are three priorities to select from:

- Urgent
- Normal
- Low

As shown in the next screenshot, just click the priority that is relevant for what we have flagged for follow up; in the following screenshot **Normal** priority has been selected:

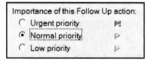

Optional follow up settings

In the **Enter a Follow Up Action**, we can add comments relevant to the follow up required for the message. I use this area in the same way I would add a Post-it note to add some comments or actions to something I am working on. It is great when we are going on leave and we can't finish off all of the messages. Just add comments in the **Enter a Follow Up Action** and, when we get back after a well-earned break, we will be able to look at the comments to refresh our memory as to the status or action required. If we have to share our job with someone or manage an individual's mail, we can add comments so that the person knows the status of the follow up and we can let them know what they need to do without having to send them a separate message about it. In our busy lives, adding comments to a message that we can't deal with there and then is a great advantage.

Other follow up settings available to us are:

- **When to Follow Up**: This option helps us to specify a follow up date and, optionally, a follow up time—I love alarms and I use this option often. I also like to see the due date for each follow up so that I can manage my time. It is like a "To Do" list or "Priority" list of messages I need to deal with.

- **Play sound**: This option is for those who set an alarm. Using this option, we can select a sound to play when the alarm goes off. Click the speaker icon to test the selected sound. We might want to select a separate sound for different priorities or have a sound dedicated just for follow ups.

- **Send e-mail notification with subject**: This option will send an e-mail when the alarm goes off. It is a great option if we want to remind someone else that something needs to be followed up. Make sure to type the addresses of those we want to receive the notification in the **Recipients** field. Click the address book icon to select names from a directory. I know lots of people who send a message to themselves to remind them that they have to follow up a message!

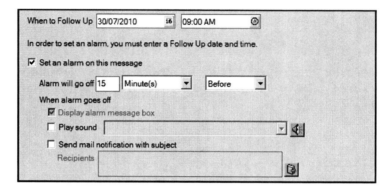

 At any time, we can edit the flag options. I sometimes do this to change the due by date or to add additional comments in the **Enter Follow Up Action** field. For example, I might have rung the person and been told they are on leave. I would change the due date to be a couple of days after they return and add comments noting the date I rang and that they are currently on leave.

Quick Flag

The **Quick Flag** option allows us to quickly add a flag with preset options. To add a Quick Flag, we have the following options:

- Select a message(s) then click the flag icon above the message list as shown next:

- Select a message(s) and then click the flag icon above the message list and select **Quick Flag**:

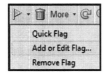

- Select a message(s), and then right-click and select **Quick Flag**:

- From within a message, click the flag icon in the row of buttons above the e-mail header.

Setting Follow Up Preferences for the Quick Flag option

The Quick Flag has similar options available that we have when we add a flag. We can follow the instructions given next to set this preference:

1. If necessary, open mail.

2. Click on **More** above the message list, select **Preferences**, and then the **Follow Up** tab.

3. For **Priority**, select a priority to display when we flag a message.

4. Check **Set follow-up date**, type a number, and select **day(s), month(s)**, or **year(s)** to set a default follow up date. To add a follow up time, select **Set follow-up time** and select a time of day.

5. Check **Set an alarm to go off** and then type a number. Select **Day(s), Hour(s)**, or **Minute(s)**, and select **Before** or **After** to set the amount of time before or after the follow up date or time to trigger the alarm. Then do any of the following:

    ° To apply the default alarm settings when we use the **Quick Flag** feature, check **Use alarm settings for Quick Flag**.

○ To play a sound when the alarm goes off, check **Play sound** and select a sound to play from the drop-down list. Click the speaker icon to test the selected sound.

○ To send an e-mail when the alarm goes off, check **Send e-mail notification to** and type the addresses of those who should receive the notification. Click the address book icon to select names from a directory.

6. Click **OK**.

 For alarms to work with follow up flags, we must first enable them in our preferences. Go to **File | Preferences | Calendar and To Do**, select the **Alarms** tab and check **Display alarm notifications**, and then click **OK**.

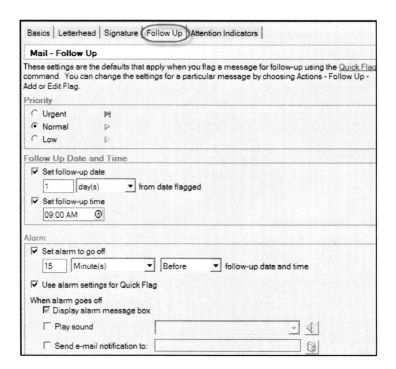

Follow Up view and Mini view

The **Follow Up** view is positioned under **Sent**. We can drag messages to this folder to add a follow up flag or we can open this view to manage our follow ups. From within this area, we can sort our columns, open or preview the message(s) that have been flagged, edit the flag, and remove the flag.

The Follow Up Mini view is always in the line of sight as it displays in the bottom of the navigator on the left-hand side of our mail file, which is an invaluable feature.

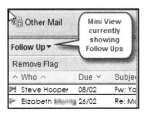

From within this area, we can sort our columns, open the message that has been flagged, edit the flag, and remove the flag:

- We can display all of the columns for a message by moving the cursor over the message. Alternatively, we can resize this window.

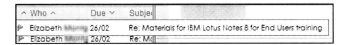

- We can open the message by double-clicking it.

- We can remove the message from the Mini View and Follow Up view (once you have completed the action) by clicking **Remove Flag**. The message stays in other mail views or folders, but no longer has a follow up flag.

- In the Mini View we can resize the view and columns:
  - Resize the Mini View Vertically by dragging the area above the words **Follow Up**.
  - Resize the Mini View Horizontally by dragging its right edge.
  - Resize the Columns by dragging the column dividers.
  - Reorder the columns by dragging and dropping the column headers.

With the mini view we can choose to display meeting notices and To Dos, and not display Follow Up messages if we prefer. We can switch to the display **New Notices** (Calendar notices such as invites or acceptance and so on) or **To Do** by clicking the down arrow beside the words **Follow Up**.

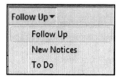

In the mini view, there is a column dedicated to the priority flag icon. We will see this column in our Inbox and other views in our mail, as well where we can see the priority icon. We can then click on the column header to group all our priorities together; this will group all our high priority follow ups to the top of the list.

Allowing delegates to add follow up flags when managing our mail

We can give delegates (typically personal assistants) the ability to add follow up flags on our behalf within our mail. This option is enabled within **Access & Delegation | Mail Preferences**. Delegates must be given **Read, edit, and create any document, send mail, enable Out-of-Office** access or higher.

 When I flag a message that is in my inbox I then file it into one of my folders. I can access the message from either the Follow Up view or the Mini view so it is not necessary to keep it in the inbox—a great option for keeping the size of one's inbox to a minimum.

 When we display conversations, we can flag conversations for follow up action and, when we do, the flag is added to each message in the conversation.

Removing flags

There are several ways to remove a flag from an e-mail. The obvious action, if one has completed the follow up action and no longer requires the e-mail, is to simply delete it! In the Mini view, click the **Remove Flag** button.

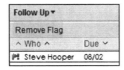

Alternatively from any view or folder or from within the e-mail, select the Follow Up button and then select **Remove Flag** as shown next:

Stationery

Stationery in Lotus Notes is a similar concept to templates in Microsoft Word, we can create a message that has information in it that we will reuse. For example many HR departments have a standard message they send to announce job vacancies. The IT department may send out a standard message announcing server outage, among other reasons. The information in these messages is predominately the same. For example, the server outage memo would have a different server name and date but the other information such as the value in the To and Subject fields would remain the same. Therefore using stationery in these instances saves us from having to recreate the message each time. I have come across quite a few people who have created Stationery to send when they are booking flights or accommodation. The stationery includes their frequent flyer information as well as passport details and so on. They typically will also include a table with headings such as Date, Time, Depart From, Arrive At, and so on so that when they are requesting flights they simply just enter details and tab through the table.

We can create stationery with text or graphics and include a recipient list that we can reuse.

[

If the Stationery includes an attachment, we can edit the attachment each time we need to send the stationery.
]

Creating stationery

To create stationery is very simple. There are three options, which are as follows:

Option 1:

1. Create a message and add required text, recipient list (if necessary), delivery options, and any other elements we require in the message.

2. From the **More** button, select **Save as Stationery**; we will see a prompt requesting a name for the stationery.

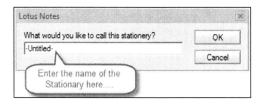

3. Type in name and click the **OK** button (or press the *Enter* key).
4. Stationery will be saved in the **Stationery** folder.

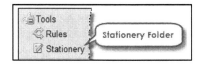

Option 2:

1. In the mail side navigator, expand **Tools** and then select **Stationery**.
2. Click **New Stationery | Message**.
3. Add required text, recipient list (if necessary), delivery options, and any other elements we require in the message.
4. Click **Save**, type a name for the stationery, and then click **OK**.

Option 3:

1. In the mail side navigator, expand **Tools** and then select **Stationery**.
2. Click **New Stationery | Personal**.
3. Between the first set of brackets under **Header**, insert any text or graphics to show at the top of the message. Note that importing is the best way to include graphics.
4. Between the set of red brackets, insert any text or graphics to show directly before the body of the message.

5. Between the last set of brackets, insert any text or graphics to show at the bottom of the page. If we want to add our signature to this field, we can insert it between the red brackets and then cut and paste it between the last set of brackets.

6. Click **Save**, type a name for the stationery, and then click **OK**.

Of all the three options, I personally prefer option one.

Editing, renaming, or deleting stationery

Often we need to tweak the stationery that we have created. We may need to change the recipient list or add a new section to the body of the memo. Other times we may need to delete stationery as it is not longer required or we may need to rename stationery.

The following are steps we need to follow to edit, rename, or delete stationery:

1. In the mail side navigator, expand **Tools** and then select **Stationery**.

2. Select the stationery to change.

3. Perform any one of the following:
   - Click **Edit**, make changes to the stationery, and then click **Save**.
   - Click **Rename**, type a new name for the stationery, and then click **OK**.
   - Click the trash icon to delete the stationery.

How to use stationery

Once we have created our stationery, we will find it very easy to use. Stationery is stored in the **Stationery** folder. To use stationery, we can go to the **Stationery** folder and double-click on the stationery we require. Alternatively, if we are in our inbox, we can click the **More** button and select **New Message with Stationery**; this will open a prompt box listing the stationery stored in the **Stationery** folder, we need to select the Stationery we require.

Bookmarking stationery

Stationery that is most often used can be bookmarked so it can be easily accessed. We can do this by opening the stationery message and then dragging the window tab of the opened stationery to the **Open** button or the **Bookmark Bar**. This will result in the stationery being listed in our **Open** button or the **Bookmark Bar**. The following screenshot shows that I have bookmarked the **Travel request** stationery. When I need to use the **Travel request** stationery, I simply click to open it from the **Open** button or the **Bookmark Bar**.

If we find ourself searching for the last e-mail we sent to a person(s), copying the contents to the clipboard, pasting it into a new memo, making some slight changes and then sending it on a regular basis, it is time we think about using stationery!

Message recall

It happens at times that we send an e-mail and then immediately realize that we have either sent it to the wrong person, have forgotten the attachment, or just should not have sent it! We can recall a message that we have sent and saved. This is useful if we sent a message when it was still not ready to be sent, or if we want to edit the content of a sent message and resend it. Be aware that some organizations may have disabled this feature and the **Recall Message** button will not be available to us.

How to recall a message

If we find that we have sent a message that we need to recall, follow the steps given here:

1. In our mail, open **Sent** or All Documents.

2. Select the message that we want to recall.

3. Above the message list, click the **Recall Message** button or alternatively the recall option is available by clicking the **More** button and then **Recall Message…**option. Remember if this button does not get displayed, then the IT Department has potentially disabled this feature.

4. If the message was sent to more than one recipient, select the recipients to recall the message from, by checking or unchecking the names displayed.

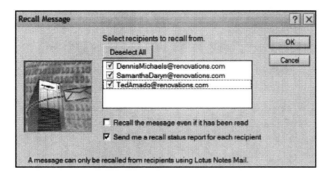

5. To recall the message from a recipient even if the recipient has already opened or previewed it, select **Recall the message even if it has been read**. Note that many IT Departments allow messages that have *not* been read to be recalled, so that even though this option is available to be selected, it will not recall the message if this option is not allowed. This is an optional step.

6. (Optional) To suppress recall status reports, check the **Send me a recall status report for each recipient** option. Recall status reports confirm whether or not a message is recalled successfully.

7. Click **OK**.

For a message recall to work, both we and the message recipient must be using Lotus Notes 8 client, mail template, and mail server. The message recipient must have the basic mail preference **Allow others to recall mail sent to me** selected. If messages are being sent externally from our organization, message recall is not possible as message recall only works internally within an organization.

If we were prompted to save the message when we clicked the **Send** button and we selected **No**, we will not be able to recall that message as it has not been saved in our Sent view or All Documents.

Spell check

Spelling is not my forte and I have to confess I love the spell check feature and use it all the time. There are quite a few options that we can set for how we want the spell check feature to operate. First, we can set a preference to spell check all our messages, we can then set our default dictionary, how we handle numbers and case, and we can select additional dictionaries. There is also the option to enable the instant spell check that identifies misspelled words as we type.

Enabling spell check for messages

We can have Lotus Notes automatically spell check all messages before sending them, or we can alternatively manually check for spelling mistakes in a message. We can also enable the instant spell checker that shows misspelled words as we type. We discussed the Instant Spell check in *Chapter 5, Mastering Lotus Notes Mail*; in this chapter we will look at the other spell check options.

Performing a manual spell check

Create a message to test the steps given next:

1. With the message open, select the text in the body of the message that we want to check the spelling of.

2. Select **Tools | Spell Check...**. When Notes doesn't recognize a word, Notes displays the **Spell Check** dialog box.

Performing spell check as we type (Instant Spell check)

Create a message to test the steps given next:

1. While the message is open, select **Tools | Instant Spell Check...**. When Notes doesn't recognize a word, the word will be identified with a red squiggly line underneath.
2. Right-click on the misspelled word; we will see alternative suggestions for spelling as well as options to add the word to the dictionary or skip it.

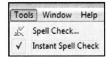

Performing an automatic spell check

In this case, Notes checks the spelling when we send the message.

1. Select **File | Preferences**, click **Mail**, and then click the **Basics** tab.

2. Select **Spell-check messages before sending**.

3. Click **OK**.

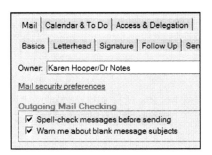

 We can enable the Instant Spell Check and the option to spell check messages before sending automatically. This will show us misspelled words as we type as well as prompts to correct any that we have missed when we send the message.

We shouldn't forget to add to our signature to the dictionary. If we don't, every time we send a message and we have the spell check option enabled, it will spell check our name and whatever we have added to our signature. Select the button **Add to Dictionary** in the **Spell Check** dialog box if parts of your signature are picked up by the spell checker.

Setting spell check preferences

As mentioned, there are different spell check options that we can select to customize the spell checker.

1. Click **File | Preferences**.

2. Click **Spell Check**.

3. Set any of the following options:

    ○   Select the language dictionary from the **Primary Dictionary** list, and then click **Set as Default**.

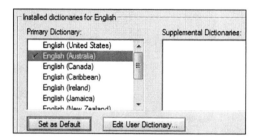

    ○   Select the **Supplemental Dictionaries** option, wherein we may see supplementary dictionaries that we can select. This will need to be installed by our IT Department.

    ○   The **Edit User Dictionary** option lists all the words we have added to our dictionary such as our name, company name, product names, and abbreviations we use. We can edit this dictionary from within Preferences or from within the Spell Check dialog box when prompted. From within this area, we can **Add** a new word by typing in the **New/Selected word** field and then clicking the **Add** button. We can also select a word such as **Admin** in the diagram and change the spelling and then click the **Update** button. Finally, we can delete a word in our user dictionary by selecting a word in the list and then clicking the **Delete** button.

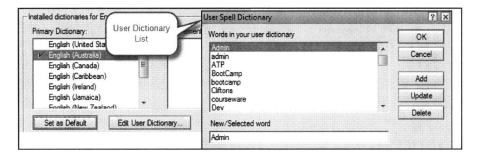

- ° There is an **Ignore words that contain numbers** option. This is a great option for those who work with part or model numbers for products where the part or model numbers that contain letters and numbers. We can also set **Ignore words that are in uppercase**.

- ° We also have an option for multi-language documents — **Keep on the fly dictionary changes until next language tag change**.

- ° **Selecting Enable Instant Spell checking** option highlights misspelled words with a red squiggly line underneath them.

- ° Under **Instant Corrections**, we can select the typical typing errors we want corrected automatically.

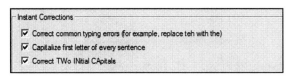

4. Click **OK**.

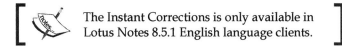

The Instant Corrections is only available in Lotus Notes 8.5.1 English language clients.

Out of office

Whenever we take annual leave, or we are away from the office, it is important to enable our Out of Office. When a colleague or customer sends us an e-mail, they get notified that we are not available with dates of when we are away, and more importantly, when we will be back in the office. In Lotus Notes 8.5, the notification of our absence is sent immediately.

I actually use my Out of Office not just for when I am on leave. I will enable it if I am training for the day as usually I can't get to my e-mails until later that day or the next day. I also enable it when I go to conferences or other business outings. We can edit our Out of Office to send a customized message for each occasion that we are away. The notification service sends replies only between the leaving and returning times we specify and sends one reply to each sender.

Enabling the Out of Office feature

The following are steps to enable this feature:

1. From within Mail or Calendar, click the **More** button and then select **Out of Office....**

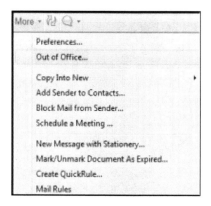

2. Enter the **Leaving** date and the **Returning** date. If we are leaving for less than a day, check **Specify hours** and enter the hours that we will be away. Depending on our organization's server configuration, we may or may not be able to select hours and may only be able to select dates. Check **I am unavailable for meetings** to show others that we are not available at these times for meetings and other related activities.

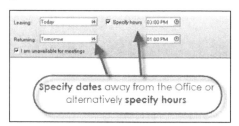

3. On the **Standard Notification** tab, edit the **Subject** field if required, and select **Append return date to subject** so the sender can clearly see when we are returning. In the **Additional body text,** add any further details such as the occasion for our absence or contact details of a person who is filling in for us while we are away. To clear this field, we can click the **Reset Defaults** button above the **Subject** field and add new details.

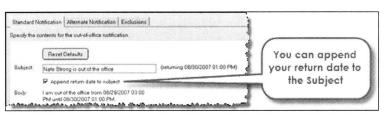

4. If you want to send an alternative notification select the **Alternate Notification** tab to send an alternate out of office notification to certain people, or to people from certain domains (such as @sampledomain.com). Specify the people and domains in the **To** field. Then specify the contents of the alternate notification.

5. Click the **Exclusions** tab to cancel the out of office notification when certain conditions are met if required. Specify the conditions we require in the relevant fields. There is an option here to prevent replies from going to messages received from the Internet. Check **Do not automatically reply to mail from Internet addresses** if this is our preference.

6. Click **Enable and Close** or, if we have already enabled the out of office notification but changed some out of office settings, click **Save and Close**.

How to disable the Out of Office feature (if necessary)

By default the Out of Office feature will automatically disabled itself; however, in some organizations, we will be required to disable the Out of Office manually as it has not been enabled to run as a service. If we do need to disable it ourselves, the Out of Office will send us a reminder to do so.

1. Open mail or calendar.
2. Above the message list, click **More | Out of Office**.
3. Click **Disable and Close**.

Duration of absence:
The shortest time is one hour. The minimum day is one. We cannot have 1 day and 4 hours. We must select either time or dates.

We can allow a delegate of our mail to enable the Out of Office notifications. In the **Access & Delegation** section of our mail file preferences, select the **Mail, Calendar, To Do and Contacts** components and then give access to **Read, edit, and create any document, send mail, enable Out-of-Office** or higher.

Junk mail

Many times we receive unwanted e-mails. We can block these e-mails by adding them to the Junk; this function is called **Block Mail from Sender**. This feature allows us to filter incoming messages and move those from specific senders directly to Junk so that they bypass our inbox. We can use this function in all mail views and folders except for **Sent, Rules, Stationery**, and **Follow Up**. Mail in Junk will need to be deleted manually.

Managing junk mails

Follow the steps below to add mail to Junk.

1. Open mail, select a message from a sender whose messages we want to add to Junk.

2. From within the inbox, click the **More** button and select **Deliver Sender's Mail to Junk**. The **Junk Mail Senders List** dialog box will open as shown in the next screenshot. Select if we want to block the mail from the individual sender or mail from any address that ends with the sender's domain.

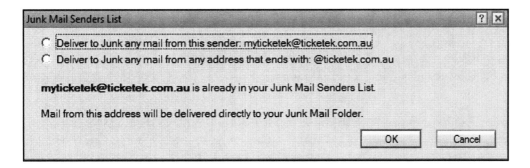

3. Click **OK**. The messages from this sender will now go directly to **Junk** located in the side navigator as highlighted here:

4. To unblock, from within **Junk**, select the **Manage Junk Mail Senders List** button; this opens the **Junk Mail Senders List** dialog box and we can select a name to remove or click the **Remove All** button. We can delete the e-mail in **Junk** however the sender's details will remain in the **Junk Mail Senders List**.

 We can also manage Junk mail from the Rules folder, which we will look at in the next section.

Rules

Often our inboxes get inundated with messages and it can be quite overwhelming. A way to prevent this is to manage our mail with rules. We can use mail rules to act automatically on new messages we receive that meet certain conditions. We can create a rule that checks for messages from a certain sender or that contains a certain subject and automatically move the messages to a certain folder, send copies of the messages to someone, or delete unwanted messages before we ever see them in our inbox. For example, I subscribe to several websites and I have set up rules to move the incoming newsletters from these websites directly to a folder so that they bypass my inbox.

The mail rules we create are stored in the **Rules** folder in our mail file. We can go there to add new rules as well as edit the ones we've created. We can edit rules, change their order so that one rule has priority over another, turn them off when we don't want to use them, or delete them entirely.

We can access **Rules** in the side navigator under **Tools**.

There is a **Quick Rule** option, which is an abbreviated set of the most commonly used rule configurations that can quickly be applied—hence the name **Quick Rule**.

The following table explains some of the **Quick Rules** and **Rules** settings for our reference:

Condition	Definition
Contains	**Contains** looks for a partial match. For example, if we have selected the rule to act on messages that contain sales in the subject, it will act on a message that has *sales conference* as well as *sales enquiry* in the subject field.
Does not contain	We will need to be careful with this as the setting is the complete opposite to the **contains** condition and is usually used in conjunction with *contains* or *is*.
Is	**Is** looks for an exact match. In our sales example, it will only act on messages with sales and sales only in the subject.
Is not	Is similar to **does not contain** but it looks for an exact match.

Creating a quick rule

Follow the steps next to create a quick rule:

1. Open mail and select a message that we would like to apply a quick rule to.

2. Select **More | Create QuickRule**.

3. As the Quick Rule is based on information in the selected message, we will see values in the **Sender**, **Subject**, and **Domain** fields. We can edit these values if necessary. The fields could be empty if, for example, we select a message that doesn't have text in the subject field.

4. There are three steps to complete the rule. With each condition we can specify any of the following states for each field value—**contains**, **does not contain**, **is**, and **is not**.

   i. We first need to select the condition to match. There are three conditions to configure—**Sender**, **Domain**, and **Subject**. We can select one of these conditions or all three.

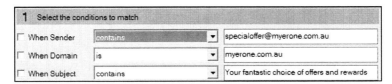

   ii. We need to decide when to take action—on one or all selected conditions.

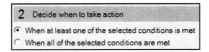

   iii. **Choose an action to perform**:

   - **Move to Folder**: We will need to select the folder we want the messages to be moved to.

   - **Change importance to High**: This option adds the red exclamation mark icon to messages to indicate the message is of high importance.

   - **Do not accept message**: This deletes the message. Note the message is not stored in **Trash** and cannot be restored.

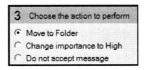

5. Click **OK** to save the configurations. The new quick rule is created and stored in the **Tools | Rules** folder. The new quick rule acts on incoming messages, but existing messages in the inbox that meet the conditions of the rule are not affected.

If the Quick Rules do not give enough options, we can create a rule.

Creating a rule

Rules have many more options to configure and are quite powerful as there are further actions we can select from and more configurations including exceptions.

1. In the side navigation pane of mail, go to **Tools | Rules** or alternatively click the **More** button and then select **Mail Rule**. This will open up the **Rules** folder.

2. In the **Rules** folder, click **New Rule**.

3. In the **New Rule** dialog box, there are two areas that we need to configure. In the first area, we need to specify conditions. Rules have several conditions that we can configure.

Condition to check	Options	Additional options
Sender	Contains, does not contain, Is & Is not	
Subject	Contains, does not contain, Is & Is not	
Body	Contains, does not contain, Is & Is not	
Importance	Contains, does not contain, Is & Is not	High, normal, low
Delivery priority	Contains, does not contain, Is & Is not	High, normal, low
To, cc, bcc & To and cc	Contains, does not contain, Is & Is not	
Body or Subject	Contains, does not contain, Is & Is not	
Internet domain	Contains, does not contain, Is & Is not	
Size	Is less than, is greater than, is, is not	
Form	Contains, does not contain, Is & Is not	Note: an example of a form is the memo form

Condition to check	Options	Additional options
Blacklist, whitelist	Contains, does not contain, Is & Is not	
All documents	None available	

 The **all documents** condition lets us perform an action on all messages that arrive in our mail while the rule is enabled. For example, we might select **all documents** and specify sending a copy of all e-mails we receive to an alternate e-mail address while we are out of the office.

4. Once we have added one condition, we can add further conditions and/or exceptions.

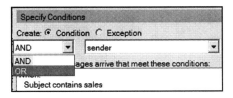

5. We can, at any time, **Remove** or **Remove All** conditions using the buttons on the right-hand side of the screen.

 Do not use quotation marks when adding text we want to check against. Text is not case sensitive.

6. Once we have entered the conditions, the next step is to **Specify Action**. Rules have several actions available and we can add more than one. The actions available are listed here:

Action	Options	Additional options
Move to folder	Select the folder to move to	
Copy to folder	Select the folder to copy to	
Send copy to	Full or header only	Enter names to send to
Set expiry date	Number	Day(s), week(s), month(s), year(s)

Action	Options	Additional options
Change importance to	High, normal, low	
Stop processing	None available	
Delete (don't accept message)	None available	

> **Send copy to** is a great option for allowing another person to manage our mail while we are out of the office. They receive a copy of the message and we still receive the original mail.

7. Click **Add Action**.
8. Click **OK** to close the dialog box; the rule is now enabled.

As we can see from the options, rules are quite extensive. Once created, rules act in the order they appear (top to bottom) in the **Rules** folder. We can change the order of the rules by using the buttons at the top of the **Rules** folder by moving them up or down.

We can edit or disable a rule at any time as well as delete the rule if it is no longer required.

Mail size indicators and quotas

In some organizations, mail administrators may set a quota to assist in managing the size of people's mail. If a quota is set and our mail becomes larger than the set limit, we will see warning messages letting us know we have exceeded our quota. In addition, new mail sent to us may be delayed, and we may not be able to save sent mails until we have reduced the size of our mail to below our quota. If quotas are enabled, we will see an indicator in the top left-hand side of our mail as shown in the next screenshots.

When we access our mail stored on a server, the Mail Quota Status indicator is displayed as a thermometer.

When we access a local replica, the Mail Quota Status indicator displays as an envelope overlapped by a thermometer:

Hovering over either indicator displays a summary consisting of a thermometer, the current mail database size and quota, and the mail server name:

Hints on reducing the size of our mail

Managing mail can be a chore. Following are some tips that may help reduce the size of our mail.

- **Delete mail**: Sort individual mail folders and views by size to identify and delete the largest messages no longer required a great place to do this is in All Documents as it encompasses all Sent, filed and received messages. After deleting messages, make sure that you go to the Trash folder and empty the trash.

- **Archive mail**: If archiving is enabled, archive messages that are no longer active. Archiving is discussed later in this chapter.

- **Change preference for saving sent mail**: If our preference for saving sent mail is set to **Always**, we may be saving many sent messages unnecessarily as every message we send is saved in our mail. Consider changing the setting to **Always prompt**, so we will be prompted each time we send a message as to whether we want to save it. If we select No, the message will not be accessible in our mail. If we select the Send and File option when sending messages the message will automatically be saved.

- **File attachment settings**:
  - Use the **Reply with History only** option that removes the attachments but keeps the original text when we reply to messages containing file attachments.
  - To prevent receiving large attachments in messages, we can create a rule to specify if the size (in bytes) **is greater than** (the number we choose) then delete.

Archiving

Archiving, as mentioned above, is a great solution for assisting in decreasing the size of our mail. When we set up archiving it creates a copy of our current mail application and stores it locally on our computer. It creates a new directory in Windows Explorer called Archive. If we ever need to take a backup of the archive application, we will find it in the IBM\Lotus Notes\Data\Archive directory in Windows Explorer if the naming conventions have been kept as the default.

We can access the archive database from our mail file in the side navigator as shown here:

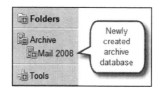

To open our archives, expand **Archive** in the side navigator and then select the archive we want to open. In the above screen shot the only archive available is **Mail 2008**. Once opened, the archive application is almost the same as our current mail excluding all the e-mails! It does look slightly different as the archive application is a yellow color and has a different title as we can see in the next screenshot:

Before we can archive, we must configure the archive settings, which we will go through shortly. We can have more than one archive database. Some people have an archive database for each year. Others prefer to only have one archive database. A consideration for how many archives we have would be size. If we want to back up our archive applications, we might need to control the size, therefore requiring us to have more than one.

Setting up archiving

Setting up archiving is quite simple, follow the steps given next:

1. Access the archive menu choices under **Action | Archive | Settings....**

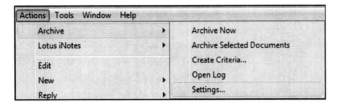

2. Click the **Create...** button on the right-hand side.

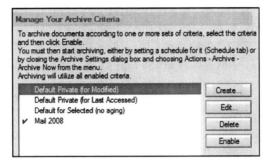

3. This will open the **Create Archive Criteria** dialog box. From within here, we have four sections that need to be complete:

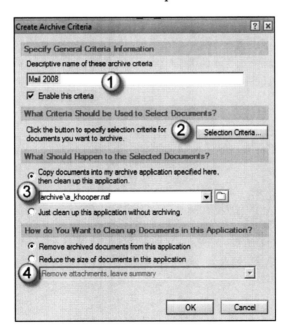

i. Give a descriptive name for the archive database and check **Enable this criteria**. Enabling the criteria shows the link to the new archive in the mail side navigator as per our example, **Mail 2008** in the screen shot earlier.

ii. Click the **Selection Criteria...** button to determine how often and which documents we want to archive. The default is **Not modified in more than 365 days**. We can change these options.

iii. We then need to decide **What should happen with the selected documents**. The default is to **Copy documents into my archive application specified here, then clean up this application**. The other option is to **Just clean up this application without archiving** however this is not recommended as there is no way to retrieve the deleted documents if there is a need to.

iv. Finally, **How do you want to cleanup documents in this application** gives two opportunities. The first choice is to completely remove the document from our current mail so that we will be able to access the document only from the archive application. The second choice is to leave a subset or summary of the document in the current mail application. This ensures we will see the archived document in our current mail file with a blue summary icon on the archived document, which represents that the document has been archived, and either the attachment has been removed or the attachment has been removed and 40KB of text remains in the original message. The great feature about this option is that we can open the archived document in our current mail file and select **Actions | Open Archived Document**; this opens up the original message that has all the original data which is now stored in our Archive application.

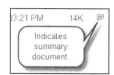

4. Click **OK** to close. We will then be prompted with the information that to use the enabled criteria we must archive either by selecting the option to **Archive Now** under the **Action\Archive** menu or clicking the **Yes** button to schedule archiving. A schedule will automate archiving at the time we allocate.

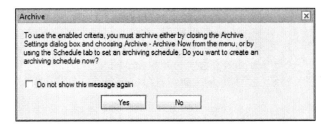

If we select not to schedule archiving by clicking on the No button, then we will need to manually archive some documents before the archive application is created.

There are four ways to archive:

- **Actions | Archive | Archive Now**: This will archive documents that meet the archive criteria.

- **Actions | Archive | Archive Selected Documents**: This archives any documents we currently have selected.

- Let schedule archiving archive according to the archive criteria.

- Drag-and-drop documents into the archive database in the side navigator.

 Recently Archived folder: We can easily find our recently archived messages by opening the **Recently Archived** folder in our archives. An archived message's subject line says **(Archived)** and the header includes the date on which the message was archived, which is very handy.

At any time we can **Edit, Delete,** or **Disable** our settings for each database by selecting the **Actions | Archive | Settings**.

In the Archive settings, we will see an **Advanced** tab as shown in the next screenshot:

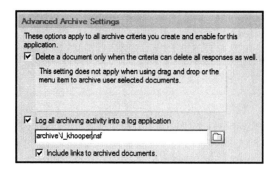

In this area, by default, archiving will delete documents only if it can delete all responses as well. An example of a response is a reply to an e-mail. By keeping this option checked, we will always be able to show the whole conversation.

There is also an option to **Log all archiving activity into a log application** option. This will give a report each time archiving occurs and can include links to the actual documents archived. The log is a separate application and is stored in the path listed in the **Advanced** tab.

Mail preferences

Throughout this chapter and the chapter before, we have set many mail preferences to configure our mail in a particular way. For example, we may have enabled the spell check to automatically check spelling when we send a memo. We also may have set up Sender Colors so that messages from certain people will be highlighted in a different color. Mail preferences can be accessed from the **File | Preferences | Mail** menu or by clicking the **More** button from within Mail and selecting **Preferences**.

Accessing mail preferences from the **File | Preferences | Mail** option gives us more areas to configure as we can set **Internet** options as well as **Sending and Receiving** preferences.

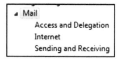

Accessing preferences from within mail using the **More** button and then selecting **Preferences** gives us the following tabs to select from:

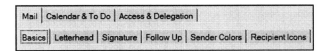

Letterhead

Throughout the chapter, as I have mentioned, we have learned how to configure most of the preferences listed on each tab in the previous screenshot. On the **Basics** tab, we had options on to we enable the spell check along with view and folder management. On the **Signature** tab, we could set up our signature to append to each memo that we send. The **Follow Up** and **Sender Colors** tabs allowed us to configure our **Quick Flag** options and color code our messages from particular senders.

The preference we have not looked at is the Letterhead. We may have noticed that when we create a message, the header of the memo will typically contain a graphic as in the following example that has the maple leaf:

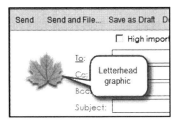

We can change this graphic by going to mail preferences and clicking on the **Letterhead** tab and browsing the different letterhead options. For each graphic that we select, to the right there is a preview screen. One of my favorites is the surfboards. We have an option to select **No Letterhead** if we prefer.

Letterhead is visible only within our organization. When a message is sent externally, the letterhead is removed or sent as an attachment. Don't forget the **No Letterhead** option if we prefer to not have the letterhead become an attachment when sending to external people.

Context menu (right-click menu)

The context menu has shortcuts to often used features such as:

- **Quick Flag**: Adds a flag to a message
- **Move to Folder...**: Allows us to file messages into folders
- **Mark as**: This gives the option to mark as Read or Unread
- **Add Sender to Contacts...**: Creates a contact of the sender in our contacts
- **Reply**: Provides reply options to the sender of the message
- **Reply to all**: Provides reply options to the sender of the message as well as those in the cc as well as bcc fields
- **Forward**: Forwards the message including history and attachments
- **Copy Into New**: Gives the option to copy the message into another message, a calendar entry, or a To Do
- **Open in New Window**: Opens the currently selected message in a new window
- **Print...**: Opens the print dialog box
- **Delete**: Moves the message to Trash

Adding tables and sections

Tables can be added to messages and documents as well as sections as described next.

Tables

Tables can be a great tool to enter data into. We can use the tab key to move from one cell to another. When I create stationery in Mail, I often use tables as I find them easier to layout my message.

The following is an example of a table that we can create in Lotus Notes. When we create a table, we can see a Table menu where we can select table properties. From within the table properties, we can select colors for the cells, cell border size and style, give a border effect such as the Drop Shadow, and even create animated tables.

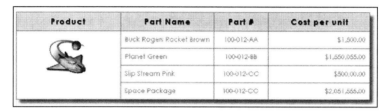

Sections

Sections help organize text within documents. For example if I was adding Policy information to a Lotus Notes document, I may want to organize the text into different paragraphs. I can then add those paragraphs to sections which will collapse the text into a heading. When the person wants to read the contents of that paragraph, they click on the heading, which expands the section. This summarizes the document and allows people to quickly identify the paragraph that is of interest to them.

Sections are either expanded or collapsed. We can also create a section within a section. The following screenshot shows the Acme Cleaning Products section being expanded.

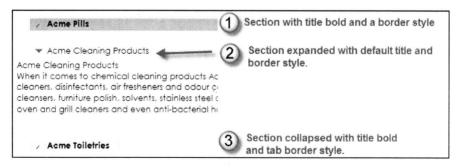

Printing documents

In Lotus Notes we can print documents and views.

1. To print, first we need to select the documents we want to print, then select **File | Print** or press *Ctrl+P*.

2. Select the printer and click the **Settings** button to select duplex options, among other things.

3. In the **What to Print** window, we can determine how we want the print to be displayed. I recommend selecting each option and clicking the **Preview** button to view.

4. The **Quality** tab allows us to select our preferred options.

5. The **Copies** option lets us select the number of copies we wish to print.

What to Print section

In the Print dialog box there is a **What to Print** section as shown in the following screenshot:

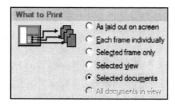

You can select any of the following options:

*   **As laid out on screen**: This will print everything that you see on the screen.

*   **Selected view**: This will print the documents as they are listed in the view. As in the example below, the Date column and the Topic column will be printed:

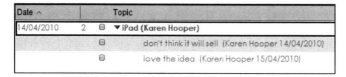

*   **Selected documents**: This will print each document selected on individual pages.

 Don't forget to preview what we are about to print.

Summary

In this chapter, we have explored the available mail tools in Lotus Notes. Many of these tools have been created to assist us in working more efficiently. For example, flagging or marking a message for follow up can assist with managing your inbox, using stationery can save time by having ready-made e-mail templates ready to go, the simple trick of adding our signature to our personal dictionary in the spell checker can save being prompted with the spell checker each time we send a message, and so on. Rules are also very powerful and are a great tool. Hopefully advantage of these tools and put them to work!

7
Managing Contacts

Contacts are a vital part of any mail system. In our working and personal lives, we can connect with numerous people and collect important contact details. In Lotus Notes, contacts can be accessed from our Mail, Calendar, To Dos, and any other Notes applications that we use to look up names. We can also open contacts directly to view or add details. It is simple to add contacts and, in this chapter, we explore how to add and manage contacts and groups (mailing or distribution lists). The topics we will cover are:

- Opening contacts
- Touring contacts
- Adding, editing, and synchronizing contacts
- Importing and exporting contacts
- Managing groups
- Contact preferences
- Allowing delegates to access our contacts
- Printing contacts

Opening contacts

When we address a message to someone or invite someone to a meeting, we can select names from the Corporate Directory or from our Contacts. Contacts can be accessed from the Open list and, from within our Contacts, we can add new contacts and enter further details for current contacts. We can also create groups, also known as mailing or distribution lists. The following diagram shows the **Open** list; we need to click on **Contacts** to open.

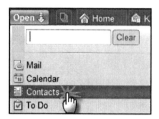

Touring contacts

Once we have opened Contacts, we will be taken to the default view of **My Contacts**. Contacts are organized in our Contacts application in different ways. The following screenshot shows the various ways we can view our contacts:

- **My Contacts**: This is where all the contacts are stored that we have added either from creating them directly or when we select the **Add Sender to Contacts** option from under the **More** button or the right-click menu in Mail.

- **Recent Contacts**: As the name suggests, **Recent Contacts** represent the people we have recently had contact with via mail or Sametime. Each time we send/receive an e-mail or chat with someone, a contact is automatically created for that person in the **Recent Contacts** view. The contact created contains their name and e-mail address. The benefit of this feature is that if we need to e-mail that person again, we simply need to start typing their name and Lotus Notes will populate the address fields from the contacts that have automatically been created in **Recent Contacts**. Often people change their e-mail address or their name. If this happens, just delete the **Recent Contact** with the old e-mail address or name, and the next time we send that person an e-mail with their new e-mail address or name, those details will be saved into our **Recent Contacts**; however, it is not possible to edit the **Recent Contact** with any further details such as a phone number however. We can promote a **Recent Contact** by clicking the **Move to My Contacts** button in the **Recent Contacts** view. Once the **Recent Contact** has been moved to **My Contacts**, we can then edit it so that we can add phone numbers or addresses. We will also be able to see this contact from iNotes (web mail) if we have access to it and see them from mobile devices if configured to work with Lotus Notes such as BlackBerrys and iPhones with Traveler.

- **Groups**: In this place, we can create, edit, and manage groups to use for mailing or distribution lists.

- **By Category**: In each contact, we have a field that we can add a category to. This enables us to categorize our contacts so that we can search by category in the **Category** view. Some of the categories I use are Medical, Restaurants, Travel, and Friends & Family. Be aware that this view is populated only if we assign a category to a contact.

- **By Company**: Each contact has a **Company Name** field; this view categorizes all contacts by the Company Name field if that field has been populated.

- **Birthday & Anniversaries**: We can add our contacts' birthdays and anniversaries and then see them sorted by date in the **Birthday & Anniversaries** view.

- **Trash**: We can drag an unwanted contact into **Trash**. We just need to use the *Delete* key on the keyboard or the **Delete** button, or last but not least, we right-click and select **Delete**. We can restore a deleted contact if we accidently deleted it. The contact stays in Trash until you empty the trash, or for a period of time we determine, in our Contacts preferences.

- **Other Contacts**: We are able to give people access to our contacts via **Preferences** in the **Mail | Access & Delegation** area. If someone has given us access to their contacts, we can open their contacts by clicking on the **Other Contacts** in the side navigator of our **Contacts**. We can then **Open other Contacts** and select the person's name in the dialog box presented. This process will open the person's contacts.

- **Advanced**: This takes us into an area that is typically managed by our IT Department. Check with our IT Department if we need to understand any of the elements in the **Advanced** area.

Show options

From within **Contacts**, we have different options on how to view our contacts. By clicking the **Show** button at the top right-hand side of our **Contacts**, we can select to preview contacts and whether we want to see contacts in a business card format or as a list. The following are the options of the **Show** button:

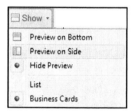

The **Business Cards** option allows us to view the contact in a similar fashion to a business card as the name implies. If we have added a graphic to the contact, we can see that graphic when we select **Show | Business Cards** as here:

If we show our contacts as a **List**, we can see the contacts as shown in the following screenshot; notice that we cannot see any graphics and it doesn't display the address.

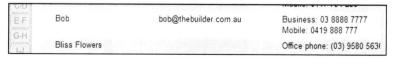

Contact view actions

There are several action buttons available at the top of the Contacts views. From within Contacts, if we right-click, we will see many of the same options available. Each button is described with its corresponding number written below.

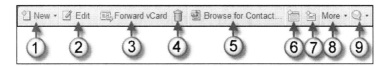

1. **New**: Click to create a new **Contact, Group, Message, Meeting, Appointment, Reminder, To Do**.

2. **Edit**: Select a contact and click the **Edit** button to edit the contact.

3. **Forward vCard**: Select a contact e-mail and vCard file with the details of the contact we have selected. We discuss vCards later in this chapter.

4. **Trash**: This is the icon for Trash; click to delete the selected contact and place in Trash.

5. **Browse for Contact**: Click to search for a particular person.

6. **Schedule a Meeting**: When we select a contact or several contacts and click **Schedule a Meeting** button, it creates a meeting invite adding the contacts into the invitees' field.

7. **Send a Message**: When we select a contact or several contacts and click the **Send a Message** button, it creates a message adding the contacts into the **To** field.

8. **More**: This action button has quite a few options.

    ○   **Preferences:** Takes us to preferences for our **Contacts**.

    ○   **Categorize**: Allows us to select one or more contacts and add a category. We can then find those contacts in the **By Category** view.

    ○   **Copy Into New Group**: Creates a mailing list from the contacts we have selected.

    ○   **Visit Web Page**: If we have added a website URL into a contact, we can select this option to view the contacts web page.

    ○   **Import Contacts**: Takes us through the steps to import contacts into our current Contacts.

    ○   **Export Contacts**: Takes us through the steps to export any of the contacts we have selected.

9. **Chat**: When clicked, the **Chat** button gives us the same right-click menu that we have in mail. The following is a screenshot of those options; check out the great **Search** options — **Google**, **Yahoo**, **Mail**, **Calendar**, **Contacts**, and **Windows Search** (if enabled):

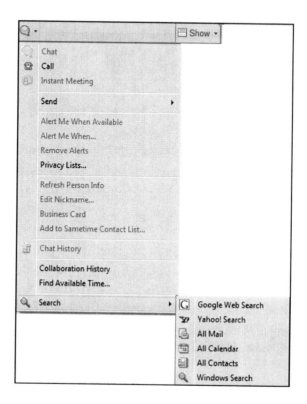

Adding, editing, and synchronizing contacts

We add contacts to save information about the people we communicate with on a regular basis. This will save us from having to search for e-mail addresses or phone numbers each time we need to contact someone. We can also print contact entries as labels, and import and export contacts as vCards.

Adding contacts

To add contacts follow the steps given here:

1. From within our mail, select a message from someone who we want to add to our contacts.
2. Click the **More** button and then **Add Sender to Contacts…**.

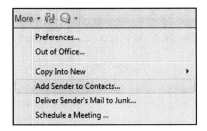

The following steps show another way to add contacts:

1. From anywhere in Lotus Notes, click the **Open** button and then select **Contacts**.
2. From within Contacts, click the **New** button and then select **Contact**.
3. Fill in fields as required.
4. Click the **Save and Close** button.

1. From within our mail, select a message from someone who we want to add to our contacts.
2. Right-click the message to view the shortcut menu.
3. Select **Add Sender to Contacts…**.

We have discovered how to create a contact. Once we create the contact, there are several fields that we can fill in. Many of these fields are self-explanatory such as **Contact Name** where we would add the contact name of the person we are adding to our Contacts. The **Company Name** field is where we would add the company name of the contact if they have one. On the contact document, we will see blue underlined field headings; the following is an example for the **Contact Name** field:

When we click on these areas, a prompt box will open with further options for each of these fields. For example, when we click the **Contact Name** field heading, the **Name Helper** dialog box is opened.

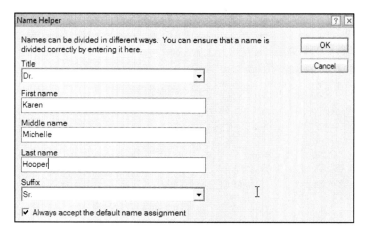

In this preceding graphic, we can see that we need to select different titles, a first, last, and middle name as well as a suffix. If we filled in all these fields, this is how the name would appear in the **Contact Name** field:

In the contact document, there are several areas with the blue underlined options. The following screenshot shows the **Company Name** options:

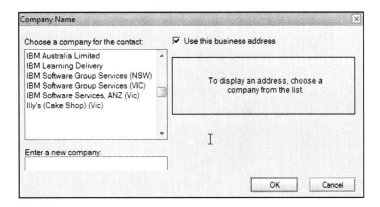

This dialog box is handy if we want to add another contact from the same company, as this gives us the choice to **Choose a company for the contact** from our current contact list and **Use this business address** to save us from having to make a double entry for the address. Alternatively, there is also the option to enter a new company.

The **E-mail** option allows us to change the labels and to select a primary e-mail address:

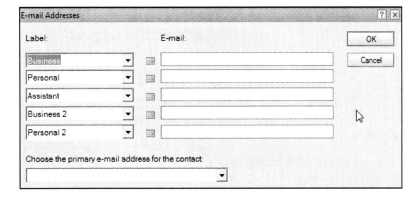

Similar choices are available for phone numbers and I find this very handy when I add a friend's details, as I can have one contact for two people but easily distinguish each individual's phone number, which is shown in the example in the following screenshot:

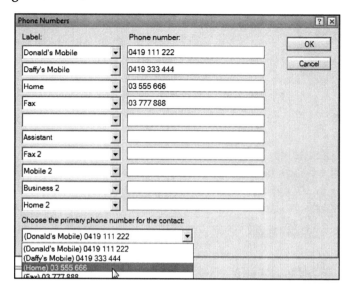

In the above example, I have changed the first label to **Donald's Mobile**, which was by default **Business**. Next, I changed the **Home** label to be **Daffy's Mobile** and changed the next label to be **Home** instead. These options will apply only to this contact. The next contact document I create will have the default choices available. Notice I have also selected the **Home** number as the primary phone number.

On the contact form, there is an **Other Information** area that gives us the options to add birthday dates, spouse's name, custom fields, and so on—worth checking out if we want to add more details to our contacts.

There are tabs at the bottom of each contact that allow us to add **Comments**, extra **Name Information** including the way the name is displayed, as well as a place where we can view certificates if we have any for that contact.

On each contact we can add a graphic by clicking the button.

 Note: The recommended size in pixels is 85w x 74h. Any image we import is automatically resized to these specifications.

Editing contacts

Often people change their details and we find it necessary to update their contacts. To update a contact, open our **Contacts**, select the contact we need to update and then click the **Edit** button. The **Edit** button is available from the **Contacts** view or from within the contact itself. A shortcut is to double-click the contact; this will open it in edit mode.

Synchronizing contacts

Synchronizing contacts is a preference that we can enable in order to get some further options. It enables us to allow others to access our contacts; this is great for co-workers or assistants. If we have been authorized to access another individual's contacts, we can also add new contacts or edit current contacts. I know quite a few assistants who manage their manager's mail, calendar, and also their contacts, so being able to easily access their contacts is a huge benefit.

If we access someone else's contacts, don't forget we can bookmark the contacts for easy access by opening the other person's contacts and then dragging that window tab to our **Open List** button. Each time we need to open that individual's contacts, we can simply select it from the **Open List** button.

Synchronizing contacts option also allows us to access our Contacts if we use iNotes, which is web mail.

Finally, if we have a smart phone such as a Blackberry, we can view and add contacts when we add a new contact on our smart phone or from within iNotes we will see that a new contact has been added to our Lotus Notes Contacts.

Follow these steps to enable the preference:

1. Go to **File | Preferences | Contacts**.
2. Check the **Enable "Synchronize Contacts" on the Replicator** option.
3. Click **OK** to save the preference change.
4. Go to the **Open** button and select **Replication and Sync**.

   Make sure the **Synchronize Contacts** is enabled with a check as follows:

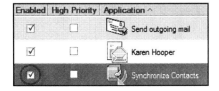

5. Click the **Start Now** button to start the synchronization.

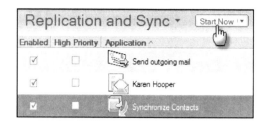

 Be aware that synchronizing contacts can impact our mail quota. The process of synchronizing actually copies our contacts into our mail on the server as, by default, our Contacts are stored locally on our machine. We discussed mail quotas as, in some organizations, mail administrators may set a quota to assist in managing the size of people's mail applications. If a quota is set and our mail becomes larger than the limit set, we will start seeing warnings that we have exceeded our quota.

Importing and exporting contacts

Contacts can last a lifetime, but unfortunately sometimes our jobs don't! Many times we may want to either import our contacts into our current place of employment or export them if we are leaving. There are a few ways that this can be done within Lotus Notes.

Forwarding contacts as vCards

A vCard file has the extension VCF and contains one or more contact entries per file. Typical fields in a vCard file are Name, Title, Phone, Fax, Address, City, State, and Zip. When we import a vCard, we import the data from these fields into matching fields in a contact document.

We may have received an e-mail from a colleague or associate that contains their vCard. We can select a contact and click the **Forward vCard** button. This creates a memo that includes a populated **Subject** field, the attachment, and instructions on how to view the attachment.

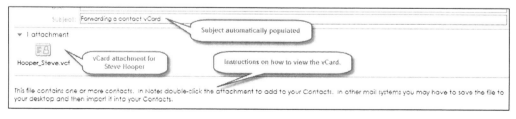

To view the vCard in Lotus Notes, simply double-click the attachment, which will open the attachment for us to view the contact details and we will also see a button to save the vCard into our Contacts. If we use another e-mail system, we may have to save the file and then import the file into that system's contact database.

Importing a vCard

Often people will send an e-mail that will include a vCard as this is a handy and convenient way to send someone all our details. Many people actually include a vCard as part of their signature. If we do receive a vCard and we want to add that person's contact details to our **Contacts**, simply double-click the vCard attachment. This will open a dialog box that shows all the contact details; we can either click **Save** or **Cancel** as per our requirement. If we select **Save**, the contact is added to our **Contacts**.

Importing contacts

We have already mentioned how we can import a vCard. We can also import files from other formats such as an Excel spreadsheet or a CSV file. To import contacts, open **Contacts** and select **File | Import Contacts**, or click the **More** button and select **Import Contacts**; we will then need to select the file you want to import. A dialog box will open that will allow us to view each contact within the file before importing. If information is appearing in the wrong place, we may have to review and adjust field mapping. To do this, click the **Map Fields** button within the dialog box. This will open a dialog box.

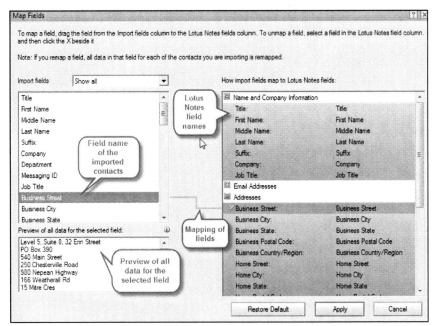

In the left-hand column, we have the field names of the fields we are importing into our **Contacts** in Lotus Notes. In the column underneath the left-hand column, we can preview the values for each field we select. In the right-hand column, we have the **Lotus Notes fields**. When we select a field in the **Import fields** column, it will highlight the field it is mapped to in the **Lotus Notes field** column. To map a field, drag it from the **Import fields** column to the **Lotus Notes field** column, and place with the field we want to map to. To unmap a field, select a field in the **Lotus Notes field** column, and then click the yellow x icon beside it. Once we are happy with the mapping, we can click the **Apply** button.

Exporting contacts

We can select one or more contacts and then either select **File | Export Contacts** or, from within the Contacts view, we can click the **More** button then select **Export Contacts**.

The **Export Contacts** dialog box will appear and we will need to select several options, including if we want to export all our contacts or just the one selected. We will also need to decide how much information we want to export. If we select **Only basic fields**, only name, e-mail, primary phone number, company, date modified, and category are included.

We will then need to select where we want to save the file and its name. When selecting the file format, for best results use vCard (vcf) for Yahoo! and IBM Lotus Notes mail clients, whereas use CSV for Google gmail and Microsoft Outlook mail clients. Note that when we export to a vCard file, only one file is created, no matter how many contacts were selected when we exported.

Under **Advance Options**, we can select if we want to **Include field names**, which is a handy option. The file can be found in the location we entered to save it.

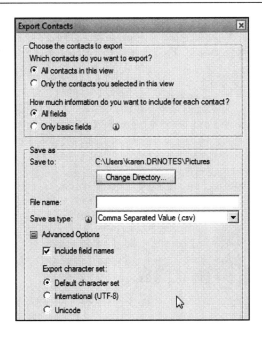

Managing groups

Often times we need to send regular messages to a particular group of people and each time have to add their names in one at a time. If we create a group and add the names of each member we send the regular message to, the next time we send that message we will only need to add the group name! **Groups**, also known as mail or distribution lists, allow us to add a group of people into one document and, each time we send an e-mail to that group, we need to reference only the group document name.

Follow the next steps to create a mailing list (group):

1. Open **Mail** or **Contacts**.
2. Click **New** and then select **Group**.
3. Enter a **Group Name**.
4. Enter a **Description**. This step is optional.
5. Click **Members** to add people or type names in directly, separating multiple entries with a comma, semicolon, or new line.
6. Enter a **Category** if required.
7. Enter information into the **Comments and Attachments** area if required.
8. Click **Save and Close**.

I always test a newly created group by creating a message and typing in the group name. Press *F9* to expand the group to confirm we have all the members necessary. The *F9* option is handy if we also want to exclude a member of the group for a particular message.

At any time we want, we can change the membership of a group or even rename the group. Simply go to the **Groups** view and then select the **Edit** button.

When we create a group, there is **Sort Member List** button that assists in viewing the members of the group as they are placed in alphabetical order. We can set this as a preference in our Contact preferences.

Contact preferences

Preferences help us manage our Contacts. We can access preferences from two areas. First is from within our Contacts by clicking the **More** button and selecting **Preferences**. The second way is **File | Preferences | Contacts**.

The available preferences are:

- **Sort the names of group members alphabetically**: This is a great choice as it is easier to view group members when they are alphabetically sorted.

- **Optimize index for advanced searching of Contacts**: This full text indexes our Contacts so that our searching is quicker and more efficient.

- **Always accept the default name assignment when adding contacts**: The default name assignment is that names are divided into first name and last name. If we add a contact whose name has three parts such as Roger El Dorado, the Name Helper displays so that we can specify "El Dorado" as the last name. Select this option to suppress the Name Helper and always accept the default name division.

- **Enable "Synchronize contacts" on the Replicator**: This option was covered in the *Synchronizing contacts* section earlier.

- **Do not automatically add names to the Recent Contacts view**: We discussed Recent Contacts in the *Touring contacts* section. This is the feature that automatically adds names of people we have either e-mailed or received an e-mail from or chatted with to our Contacts. This functionality is on by default; however, if we check this option, we can disable the feature if we prefer.

- **Delete documents in my Trash after *xx* hours:** Enter the number of hours we want to keep a contact before deleting it. The default is **48** hours.

- **Default display for contact names**: The default for displaying contact names is **First Name Last Name**. We can select another display option and select if this is for new contacts or all contacts.

- **Default address format**: Each country or region can have different address formats. We can select the different formats and see the layout of the address in these formats and which countries they apply to.

- **Create shortcuts to open the other contacts of these people**: If we have been granted access to open another person's contacts, we can add their name here and we will see a shortcut to that person's contacts in the side navigator of our contacts.

The following is the dialog box for the **Contacts Preferences**. Once we have set our preferences, click the **OK** button to save them.

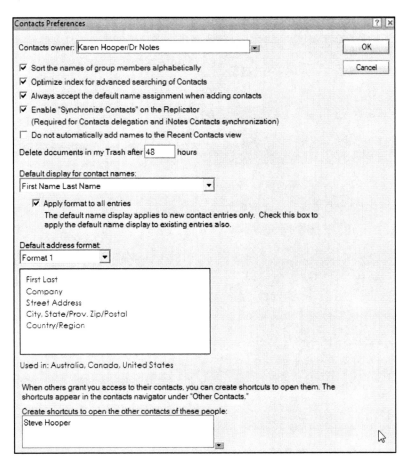

Allowing delegates to access our contacts

As we discussed in the previous section, we can have access to other people's contacts. To do this they must first allow us access. If we want others to access our contacts, we must also give them access.

This is an important feature that can really aid assistants and their managers. Assistants typically manage their manager's mail and calendar appointments and often need to ensure that their manager's contacts are up-to-date. It is also great tool for teams to be able to share contacts as they will often contact the same people.

We must have selected the preference to **Enable "Synchronize contacts" on the Replicator** in our **Contacts Preferences**. Once we select to synchronize our contacts, a copy of our contacts is placed into our Mail/Calendar and To Dos that reside on the server. This allows others to access our contacts as, without this process, our contacts are accessible only on our local computer. Be aware that if we give access, we must also give access to our mail, calendar, and To Dos, or you can just give access to calendar and To Dos.

To allow others to have access to our contacts, follow these steps:

1. Ensure that we have enabled the preference **Enable "Synchronize contacts" on the Replicator** in our **Contacts Preferences**.
2. Select **File | Preferences | Calendar and To Do** or **Mail.**
3. Select **Access and Delegation**.
4. Click the **Add** button; this will open the **Add People/Groups** dialog box.

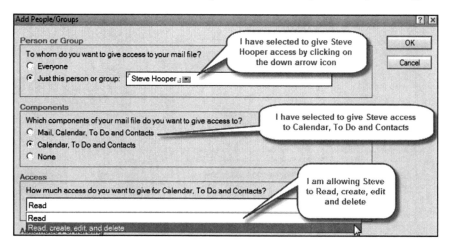

5. In the **Add People/Groups** dialog box, we need to complete three areas:

    i.   **Person or Group**: Select if we want to give **Everyone** in our organization access or just a particular person or group. If we select the later, we must select their name from the Corporate Directory by clicking on the down arrow icon.

    ii. **Components**: Select if we want to allow access to our **Mail**, **Calendar**, **To Dos**, and **Contacts**, or just our **Calendar**, **To Dos**, and **Contacts**. If we select **None**, no one will have access to our contacts.

    iii. **Access**: Here we can select whether we want the person or group to be able to read only or to create, edit, and so on.

6. Click **OK** to save these preferences.

Delegates can open other people's Contacts from their Contacts in the side navigator by selecting **Open Other Contacts....**

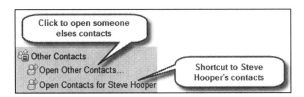

 If we have given someone access to our Contacts, remind them they can create a shortcut to our contacts in their Contacts Preferences. In the preceding screenshot, I have created a shortcut to Steve Hooper's contacts.

Printing contacts

Even though printing is frowned upon these days with people trying to be eco friendly, there are times when we need to print a particular contact or print labels, and so on. We can print our contacts as labels, print a contact entry to see all of the information about a contact or a group, or print the contact information as it appears in a view.

Printing contact entries as labels

We can print contacts as address or shipping labels in various sizes. Follow the steps given below:

1. From within **Contacts**, select the one or more contacts.

2. From the menu, click **File | Print**.

3. Select a printer if one is not selected.

4. Under **Print Style** specify the following:

    ○   **Print Style**: Address or shipping label style (each label style indicates how many labels print on a page).

    ○   **Other Options**: Depending on the address or label style we select, this field will give an option to select the size of the labels.

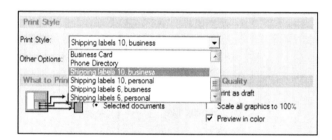

5. Under **What To Print**, select **Selected documents**.

6. Click the **Documents Style** tab.

7. Under **How to print each document**, select **Print multiple documents on each page**.

8. Under **Format Each Document Using**, select **An alternate form**, and then make the same selection we made for **Print Style** in step four.

 The label type indicates approximately how many labels we can expect to print on a continuous page, and the paper size shows the size of the labels.

9. Click the **Page Setup** tab and specify any additional page formatting that is required such as orientation and page margins.

10. Click the **Documents Style** tab to select how to print each document, label format, paper type.

11. Click **Preview** to view our print setup selections.

    Note that this and the above two steps are optional.

12. Click **OK**.

Printing a contact or group

We may be walking out the door and we need the details of the person we are about to visit! We can print an individual contact or group. Follow the steps given next:

1. From **Contacts**, do one of the following:

    ° Select one or more contacts.

    ° Click **Groups** in the navigation pane and select one or more groups.

2. Click **File | Print**.

3. Select a printer if one is not selected.

4. For **Print Style**, select from the list:

    ° **Default form**: To print contacts with headers that identify information types, similar to the Contacts entry form.

    ° **Booklet**: To print contacts in a listing, similar to an address book.

    ° **Business Card:** To print each entry as if it were a business card.

    ° **Phone Directory**: To print each entry in booklet format, but including phone numbers only.

5. Under **What to Print**, select **Selected documents** (if it is not already selected).

6. Click the **Page Setup** tab and specify additional page formatting if required.

7. Click **OK**.

Printing the Contacts view

We can print our contacts as we see them within our contacts. This gives us a "list type" printout and can be handy if we need to give someone a printed list of our contacts. We can print from the **My Contacts** view or from the **By Company** view, or even **By Categories**.

Select the contacts we want to print and then **File | Print**. In the **Print View** dialog box under **What to Print**, select **Selected View**. Click the **Preview** button to preview what we are about to print and then click **Done** to close the preview. Click **OK** to complete the printing.

If we want to include our contact addresses, select **My Contacts** and show the view in the **Business Card** format.

Summary

Our contacts are an integral part of our mail and calendar system. This chapter has assisted us in understanding how to manage our contacts. We are now set to take advantage of the features such as Recent Contacts, short cuts to adding contacts, groups, and so on. We can now also check our Contact Preferences to ensure we are happy with the settings.

8

Calendar and To Dos

Time is such an important commodity for all of us. Using tools to help us manage and organize our time is important, especially when our lives can be so full. The Lotus Notes calendar can assist us in managing our time and can be an integral part of our busy lives.

Our calendar can contain our dentist appointments, birthdays and anniversaries, reminders to pay our bills or even pick up the dry cleaning. Calendars help keep our personal lives organized and, in today's business, the calendar is a very important tool. The calendar assists us in managing our time, especially with meetings, as often in the corporate world we are very meeting driven. We can invite people, check their availability, and even find a room to meet in. There are other tools such as group calendars, calendar overlay (where we can overlay another person's calendar on our calendar), and repeating calendar entries (that really benefit us in working with others.)

To Dos, known in some other applications as **Tasks**, are great for creating an electronic To Do list. My favorite feature of To Dos is being able to assign tasks to others!

This chapter explores the calendar and To Dos in depth; the topics we will cover are:

- Calendar tour
- Using our calendar
- Adding to our calendar
- Responding to meeting invites
- Managing meetings—be the chair!
- Calendar preferences
- Rooms and resources
- Printing the calendar
- Calendar tools
- Group calendars
- To Dos

Calendar tour

Before we venture into the details of the calendar, let's take the time to explore the different areas and ways to navigate around it the calendar.

Opening the Calendar

As you may have noticed in Lotus Notes, there is typically more than one way of doing things.

To open the calendar, do one of the following:

- Click **Open** and then select **Calendar** as in the next screenshot:

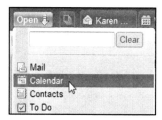

- Click the **Calendar** from the **Home** page.

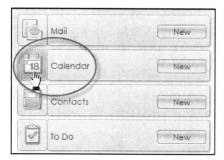

- From **Mail** or **To Do**, we can switch to the **Calendar** by clicking on the icon next to our name.

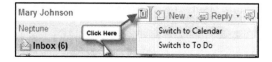

We can also see what is on our calendar in the **Day-At-A-Glance** panel in the Lotus Notes sidebar. This is a really handy option for viewing our calendar as we can be anywhere within Lotus Notes and see what is on our calendar for that day. The Day-At-A-Glance panel has already been discussed in detail in *Chapter 1, First Impressions (The Client Interface)*.

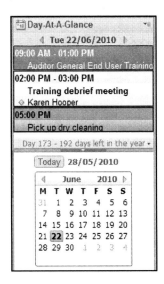

Calendar side navigator

The calendar side navigator allows us to navigate to the different areas within the calendar. The side navigator can be split into three distinct areas. First is the calendar picker, second the calendar views, and third the MiniView. First, let's look at the calendar picker.

Calendar Picker

This is located at the top left-hand corner of our side navigator. As the name suggests, it is a calendar where we can pick dates and there are some cool features that will save us time.

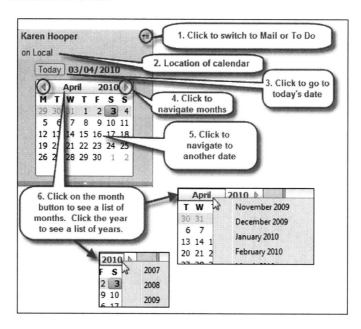

- **Click to switch to Mail or To Do (1):** When we click here, we see a choice to switch to Mail or To Do. I always find it easier to use the **Open** button though.

- **Location of calendar (2):** The location "Local" indicates our PC. If there was a name of a mail server here, it would be an indication that we are accessing our mail on a server.

- **Click to go to today's date (3):** If we have been navigating to different dates within our calendar and we want to go back to today's date, click the **Today** button.

- **Click to navigate months (4):** The left-hand arrow when clicked takes us to the previous month, whereas the right-hand button when clicked takes us to the next month.

- **Click to navigate to another date (5):** We can click on a date to change our calendar to that date.

- **Click on the month button to see a list of months. Click the year to see a list of years (6):** When we click on the month, it shows a drop-down list of other months to select from. When we click on the year, it shows a drop-down list of other years to select from.

Calendar Views

This is where we can select different views such as days, weeks, or months. The default view for the calendar is the **One Week** view. If we change to another view and open Lotus Notes, we will return to the last view that we switched to.

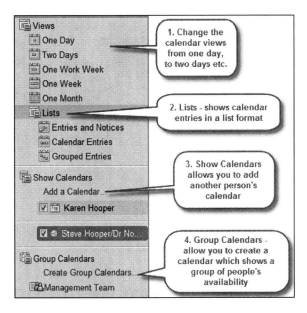

- **Views – Change the calendar views from one day to two days etc. (1)**: We have different choices on how many days we want to view in our calendar.

- **Lists – shows calendar entries in a list format (2)**: Typically when we look at our calendar, it looks similar to a paper calendar. If we select one of the options under **Lists**, we can see our calendar entries in list format.

List option	Description
Entries and Notices	Lists everything we have added to our calendar plus meeting invites and responses from invitees. We can use this area to accept a meeting we previously declined or find a meeting we have accepted, and so on.
Calendar Entries	Lists everything we have added to our calendar.
Group Entries	Groups together repeating appointments and also groups meeting invites with all the responses (acceptances or declines).

- **Show Calendars - allows you to add another person's calendar (3)**: We can overlay another calendar over our own. When adding them, we select a color and each calendar will show in the color we selected for it.

- **Group Calendars - allows you to create a calendar which shows a group of people's availability (4)**: A group calendar shows the availability of people who we have added as members of the group calendar. We will discuss group calendars later in this chapter.

MiniView

The MiniView is at the bottom of the side navigator. It has three options. It can show **Follow Up** that shows e-mails we have marked for follow up. It also gives the option of **New Notices** that shows meeting invites and responses to meetings. Finally, it can show our **To Do**.

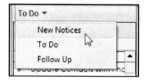

Preview, Filter, and Summary options

In this section we will explore the options we have for viewing our calendar. There are different preview options as well—for example, we can filter the calendar entries to show only meetings. My personal favorite is the **Summary** option that shows our calendar entries in an agenda-type format.

Preview options

Click on the **Show** button to enable **Preview on Bottom** or **Preview on Side**. Once enabled, we can preview our calendar entries. We can select **Hide Preview** to disable previewing.

Filter options

We can also select the option to **Filter** what is on our calendar to easily find entries.

The filter options are shown in the preceding screenshot and explained next:

- **Chair**: We can show meeting entries only where we are the **Chair**. This means we have created the meeting and invited others.

- **Type**: We can show meetings by **Type** such as showing only reminders or anniversaries.

- **Status**: When we select to filter by **Status,** we will be prompted with another dialog box to select which status we want to filter by. This option shows the status of meetings that we have:
    - **Accepted**
    - **Tentatively Accepted**
    - **Draft**

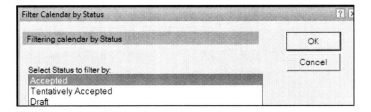

- **Private**: This option will show only calendar entries that we have marked private. A calendar entry that is marked private means that only we can see the details of the calendar entry; if we have an assistant or another person who accesses our calendar, they will not be able to see the subject or content of the calendar entry. When we create a calendar entry, we will have the option to **Mark Private**.

- **None**: Turns off the filter functionality and shows all calendar entries.

Summary options

By default, the calendar shows timeslots on every view except the **Month** and **Lists** views. There is an option to view by **Summary** that changes the calendar to show only times or days that have calendar entries. It also shows them in a list format similar to how the Blackberry shows the calendar as an Agenda or the iPhone shows the calendar as a List.

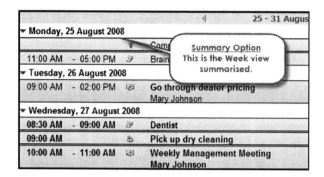

Calendar Footer

The **Calendar Footer** shows how many days, weeks, and months have passed and are left in the year. Uncheck the option to hide, check to show.

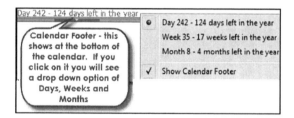

Calendar view action buttons

There are several action buttons available at the top of the calendar views. From within calendar, if we right-click, we will see many of the same options available.

New action button

When we click the **New** button, by default an appointment is created. We can change this default in Calendar Preferences. Alternatively, we can click the arrow to the right of **New** to see a drop-down list explained in the following bullet list. If we have created the calendar entry and want to change the type, click in the **Type** field and select a different option.

- **Meeting**: Where we invite others including rooms and resources if required.

- **Appointment**: We can use this option if we are not inviting others.

- **All Day Event**: As the name suggests, we can use this for events that cover the whole day such as annual leave or seminars. It only provides a choice of dates, it does not include times.

- **Anniversary**: Birthdays or anniversaries such as a wedding anniversary. Automatically repeats for 10 years. It is set to **Mark Available** so that it does not block out our time and shows our time as available if people are trying to schedule a meeting with us.

- **Reminder**: Has date and time options. Does not block out our time. Shows our time as available if people are trying to schedule a meeting with us.

- **Event Announcement**: Allows us to invite people but not receive replies from them. The invitees can add the invite to their calendar. Great for inviting people to compulsory corporate-wide meetings or events such as a company BBQ where we want to let people know about the event but we don't need to know if they are attending.

- **Message**: Creates a mail message. We can use the keyboard shortcut *Ctrl+M*.

- **Contact**: Create a person contact in our contacts.

- **Group**: Adds a group (also known as mailing list) to our contacts.

- **To Do**: Create a task in our To Do.

The following is the drop-down list of choices when we click the down arrow to the right of **New**:

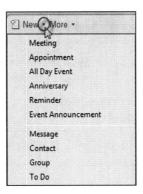

When we click the **New** button rather than the down arrow, our default calendar entry will be created; often this is a meeting or appointment. Once we have created the calendar entry, we can change the type. The following is a calendar entry with the **Type** field highlighted. Click in this field if to change the type of calendar entry we will be creating.

More action button

There are more options available when we click on the **More** button. From this menu we can select:

- **Preferences**: From this area, we can set defaults for our Calendar including setting times for our schedule, enabling alarms, setting favorite rooms, and giving access to our calendar to others.

- **Out of Office**: We can enable this to inform people of our absence. We can now allow a person whom we have given access to our mail to enable this on our behalf.

- **Import Holidays**: We need to select this option to import holidays that have been configured by our IT Department.

- **Open Person's Calendar**: Allows us to select a name so that we can open their calendar if we have been granted access.

- **Create Group Calendars**: From here we can create new group calendars or alternatively view any group calendars that we have created.

- **Calendar Cleanup**: It is a tool to assist with safely deleting past calendar entries including past repeating entries (but not future ones).

Many of these options will be explored in detail further on in this section. The Out of Office functionality has already been discussed in *Chapter 6, Lotus Notes Mail Tools*.

Adding to our calendar

Now that we have toured the calendar, our next step is to add those important dates to our calendar.

Creating a calendar entry

As we have seen, there are different types of calendar entries. The following steps take us through how to create and add them to our calendar.

1. At the top of the calendar, click the **New** button to create our default calendar entry or click the down arrow next to the **New** button and select one of the six options available. Depending on which calendar entry type we select, we will have different options available.

2. If the calendar entry created is not the one we wanted, click in the **Type** field to change it. Note, once the calendar entry has been saved or sent the calendar type cannot be changed. We would need to copy it into a new calendar entry and change the calendar type then.

3. Type a short description in the **Subject** field.

4. Depending on the entry type, specify date, time, and time zone information as necessary in the **Starts** field and, if necessary, in the **Ends** fields.

5. Some fields may be hidden in the calendar form. If required, click the **Display** button and deselect or select fields we require or do not require. The following is the **Display** button expanded:

6. Because the Meeting calendar is more complex, it has more display options as shown here:

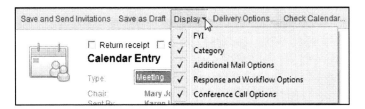

7. Enter values into the following fields if required.

   ° Click **Repeat** to create repeating calendar entries and then specify repeat options. We will cover repeating appointments further in this chapter.

○ If we have given others access to our calendar but not our mail, select **Mark Private** if we want the calendar entry to be for our eyes only. Those with access to our calendar can see the times and dates of private calendar entries but cannot see details of the entries such as the subject and description. This is a great option for planning that surprise birthday party for our assistant! Note that **Mark Private** is different from **Encrypt** as an encrypted meeting would only be able to be read by the chair and those invited. Use the encrypt option for meetings and private for all other calendar entries.

○ Select **Notify Me** to set an alarm for the entry. If we have alarms enabled, then to disable we need to click **Notify Me** and then check **Disable an alarm notification before this event occurs**.

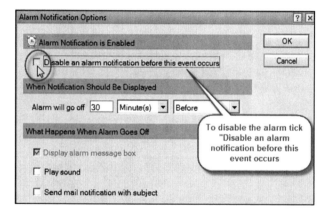

○ Select **Mark Available** to keep the entry's time free in our free time schedule. This means the time allocated for this calendar entry will not show us as being busy when people check our schedule. By default, **Anniversaries** are marked available so they do not block out our free time.

○ Select to **Sign** or **Encrypt** if required. This option may be hidden; if required click the **Display** button and select **Additional Mail Options**. Sign adds a digital signature to ensure the receiver that the entry has not been tampered with. Encrypt allows only the chair or creator of the calendar entry and the invitees to see the details of the entry.

- ° Check calendar for dates by clicking the **Check Calendar** button.

- ° Type a location in the **Location** field. This will automatically be populated with the room name for meetings that have a room invited.

- ° Select or type a category name in the **Category** field. This field can be hidden if not required by clicking the **Display** button and deselecting **Category**. In the calendar side navigator, we can view calendar entries sorted by **Category** under **Lists | Entries and Notices**; click on the **Category** column header to sort.

- ° Add any additional information about the entry such as a description or file attachments, and add to the **Description** field.

8. If the calendar entry type is **Meeting,** refer to the next section for further details. If we are creating a meeting, there are several more options available; we will discuss creating meetings later in this chapter.

9. Click **Save and Close**.

10. We may be prompted to create the entry despite a conflict with another entry or our availability preferences. Click **Yes** to create the entry or **No** to cancel creating the entry. By default, if we have something already booked in our calendar and we add another entry, we will then be prompted. We may also be prompted if the new entry falls outside of our times of availability, which we can set in calendar preferences.

 Another way to create Appointments is to use the **More...Copy Into New Calendar Entry**. This is useful when we want to copy the information from the memo into the new calendar entry.

Repeating appointments

Often we need to create an appointment, reminder, or meeting that repeats. There are many repeat options that we can select from. When we click **Repeat**, a dialog box appears and within here we can select our repeat options.

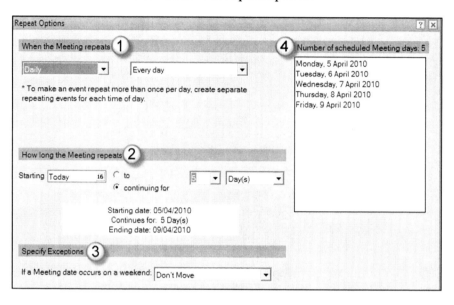

As can be seen in the preceding screenshot, the **Repeat Options** is split into the areas, which we will discuss now.

- **When the Meeting Repeats**: From here we can select the repeat interval such as **Daily**, **Weekly**, **Monthly** and, in the next field, we can select how often should we have the repeat interval such as **Daily**, **Weekly**, and so on. There is a **Custom** option that allows us to simply select the dates that we need the calendar entry to repeat on.

- **How long the Meeting repeats**: If we have selected **Daily** in the previous section, in this section we need to select for how many days, if weeks for how many weeks, and so on. In the **Number of scheduled Meeting** days section, it will show the repeating dates, which assists in knowing that we have selected the correct number of days, weeks, or months to repeat.

- **Specify Exceptions**: In this area it caters for if a repeating entry falls on a weekend. We have the following options: **Move to Friday**, **Move to Monday**, **Move to Nearest Weekday**, or **Don't Move**.

- **Number of scheduled Meeting days**: This area shows the days that the calendar entry will be repeated on. It is important to check these dates to make sure the repeating intervals are correct.

In the **When the Meeting Repeats** section, there is a **Custom** option that allows us to select the dates from a calendar. We may have to scroll to see the **Custom** option.

Changing dates on repeating calendar entries

There may be times when we need to change the details of a repeating calendar entry. Imagine we've created an appointment that repeats every Friday. We realize that Easter is coming up and we need to move the Friday meeting to the next Tuesday. We would open the Friday appointment and change the date to Tuesday. When we click on the **Save and Close**, we will be prompted with the following dialog box:

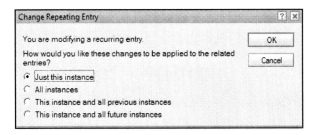

Because we are modifying a recurring calendar entry, we need to select if the change of date applies just to the entry we have changed or to all of the repeating appointments. We can also choose **This instance and all previous instances** and **This instance and all future instances**. Once we have selected an option or left it at the default which is **Just this instance**, click the **OK** button. The changes will then be applied to the effected entries. If we are changing a meeting, invitees, rooms, and resources will be updated. We need to watch for the responses from our invitees and the rooms and resources if booked. I have known of people turning up to a meeting room and finding it occupied. What they failed to notice was that the room responded as unavailable when the meeting date was changed, as they didn't take notice of the responses.

Responding to meeting invitations

Some people may not create many meetings but they may receive meeting invitations. Meetings invitations come to us via the inbox; there are several options that we can select when we respond to a meeting invite.

Responding to an invitation

It is important to respond to a meeting invitation even if it is to say you're not coming. As mentioned, meeting invitations arrive into our inbox; however, we will also see them arrive into the MiniView if we have the **New Notices option** selected. We may also see an invitation that we have not responded to on our calendar. This is because there is a preference wherein we can set to show unprocessed meetings on our calendar and they will be a gray color. If we are using the **Day-At-A-Glance** in our sidebar, we will see unprocessed meetings there as well. The following is the MiniView with the option **New Notices**:

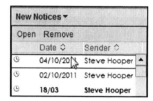

When we open the invitation, we will see options to respond.

We will now go through each of the options.

- **Accept**: When we click **Accept**, it adds the meeting to the calendar and sends an acceptance to the chair—the person who invited us.

- **Decline**: When we click **Decline**, it sends a decline notice to the person who invited us (the chair). We can set a preference to show cancelled meetings in our calendar. We will go through preferences later in this chapter.

- **Respond**: There are quite a few options under the **Respond** button.

    ° **Tentatively Accept**: Adds the invitation to our calendar with the option **Mark Available** selected and sends a tentative acceptance to the chair. If someone was to check our availability at this time, it would say that we were free.

- ○ **Propose New Time**: When we select **Propose New Time**, there will be an option to check availability. Click the **Check Availability** button to see the availability of attendees for our new proposed time. The chair must respond to the new time. If accepted, all attendees who have accepted the original meeting time, tentatively accepted, or declined, and have been asked to be kept informed, will be sent a reschedule notice. Rooms and resources will be automatically updated. The responsibility of the chair is to make sure they check the responses from all attendees including rooms and resources to make sure they can all still come. The chair can decline the new proposed time or propose another new time.

- ○ **Delegate**: This sends an invitation to the delegated person and informs the chair.

- ○ **Accept with Comments, Decline with Comments, Tentatively Accept with Comments, Propose New Time with Comments** and **Delegate with Comments**: All these options help us in adding comments with our response to the chair.

- • **Request Information**: Creates a request document that we can enter our query into, and which will be sent to the chair.

- • **Check Calendar**: Opens our calendar to the date of the invitation.

Delegating, declining an invitation and setting decline/delegate preferences

When we select to **Delegate**, there will be an option to select a delegate. Once we have added the delegate, we can click the **Check Availability** button to see the availability of our proposed delegate. The delegate will receive an invitation and the chair will receive a notification informing them of who we have delegated the meeting to. There is an option to for us to be kept informed of any updates to the meeting.

When we select to decline a meeting invitation, there is an option for us to be kept informed of any updates to the meeting. This option can be set by default in our calendar preferences.

1. In the **Calendar**, click on the **More** button and then select **Preferences**.

2. Select the **Display** tab, then the **Notices** tab.

3. Select preferences in the **Keep Me Informed** section as shown here:

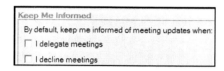

There are times when we receive an invitation and we require more information. When this occurs, we can request further information by clicking **Request Information** to ask the meeting chair for information about the meeting before responding to the invitation.

The chair receives a notice and can respond from within the request notice.

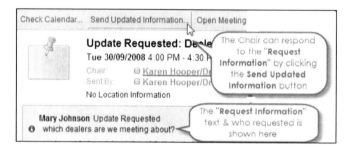

Creating meetings

Meetings have more options available as they involve inviting others as well as checking schedules. Earlier we learned how to create a calendar entry; all those steps still apply and in this section we will focus on the extra fields available in meetings.

Scheduling a meeting

The following are the instructions to create a meeting:

1. Open the calendar, click the down arrow next to the **New** button and select **Meeting**.

2. If we have given others access to our calendar, select **Mark Private** to prevent them from reading the entry. Those with access to our calendar can see the times and dates of private calendar entries but cannot see details of the entries such as the subject and description.

3. Select **Notify Me** to set an alarm for the entry, and then set alarm options.

4. Select **Mark Available** to keep the entry's time free in our schedule. This means the time allocated for this calendar entry will not show as being busy when people check our schedule. This option is not usually selected for meetings as we want our time to not be available so that we don't get double booked.

5. Type a description in the **Subject** field.

6. Specify date, time, and time zone information in the **Starts** field and, if necessary, in the **Ends** fields. The start date and end date cannot be greater than 24 hours. If we need the meeting to span more than 24 hours, we will need to create the meeting as a repeating entry.

7. If the meeting will be occurring more than once, click **Repeat** and enter repeating details.

8. We can select **Response and Workflow** options if required in our meeting. These fields may be hidden. If required, click the **Display** button and select **Response and Workflow Options**. Alternatively, these settings are available when we click the **Delivery Options** button or when we create an **Event Announcement** calendar entry.

   ○ **Do not receive responses from invitees**: This means we will not receive an acceptance or decline. The invitee can only add the meeting to their calendar as there is no option for them to accept or decline.

   ○ **Prevent counter-proposals**: This prevents an invitee from proposing a new time.

   ○ **Prevent delegation**: As the name suggests, the option to delegate is not available.

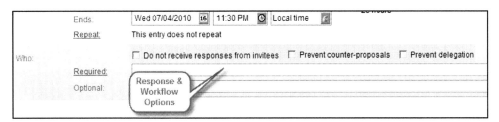

9. **Required**: Enter names of people who are required to attend the meeting. Click on **Required** to open the Corporate Directory to search for names or simply type the name of the person we want to invite in the field, using a comma to separate names.

10. **Optional**: **Required** and **Optional** invitees receive a notice that includes response options such as **Accept** and **Decline**. When we check the scheduler to suggest meeting times, it prioritizes the free time of required invitees higher than the free time of optional invitees.

11. **FYI** invitees receive a notice that does not include response options but includes the option to add the meeting to the calendar. Other invitees cannot see the names of **FYI** invitees and it is similar to the BCC functionality in e-mail.

12. If rooms have been set up within Lotus Notes in our organization, click **Rooms** and select the room we require from the Corporate Directory or click **Find Rooms**, fill in the required fields, and then click the **Search** button; select a room from the **Search Results.** We may be prompted to add the **Room** or **Site** to our preferred list.

13. If resources have been set up within Lotus Notes in our organization, click **Resources** and select the resource we require from the Corporate Directory or click **Find Resources**, select a Resource Category, fill in the required fields, and then click the **Search** button; select a room from the **Search Results.** We may be prompted to add the **Resource** or **Site** to our preferred list.

14. Click **Find Available Times** to open up the scheduler. The scheduler has two main areas — **Summary** and **Detailed**. The **Summary** option gives suggested times when everyone is available. The **Detailed** option shows a graphical representation of people's availability. We will cover the scheduler in detail further in this chapter.

15. If the meeting is an online meeting and we have Sametime enabled within our organization, click **Online Meeting**. This will open the **Reserve Online Meeting** dialog box where we can select an online meeting if there is one set up, otherwise add one by clicking the **New...** button.

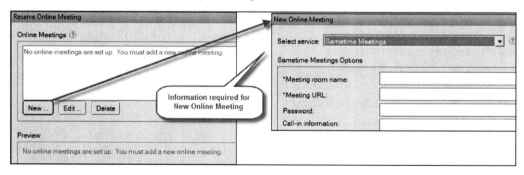

16. Click **Delivery Options** to specify delivery options for the invitation, including if we require a Return Receipt, or if we want to prevent the invitees from counter-proposing or delegating their acceptance. We can also set security options such as sign or encrypt in this area.

17. Select or type a category name in the **Category** field. This field can be hidden if not required by clicking the **Display** button and deselecting **Category**.

18. Click on the **Description** tab. Add any additional information about the meeting, such as the agenda or the purpose for meeting; we can also add attachments such as a PowerPoint presentation, and so on.

19. Select to **Sign** or **Encrypt** if required. This option can be hidden if not required by clicking the **Display** button and deselecting **Additional Mail Options**.

20. Type any general location information for the meeting in the **Location** field; however, if a room has been scheduled and accepted, the room's location will show in the **Location** field.

21. Either select **Save as a Draft** or click **Save and Send Invitations**.

22. If prompted to create the entry despite a conflict with another entry or our availability preferences, click **Yes** to create the entry or **No** to cancel creating the entry. For information on conflict checking and setting our availability preferences, see the Setting our free time schedule section.

23. Once the invitation has been sent out, we will receive responses from invitees.

Creating meeting shortcut in mail

We can also create a meeting with a person we have selected in our mail. We have discussed this in Chapter 6 under the *Finding available time* section.

1. Select a message from a person in our inbox who we want to have a meeting with.

2. Right-click on that message; we will see their name listed at the top of the right-click menu.

3. Select their name, then from the extended menu select **Find available time**.

4. The scheduler window will appear and show the first availability of the person we have selected and ourself.

5. Click **Create Meeting** or **Close**.

Reserving rooms and resources

Rooms can be varied—some are meeting rooms, some rooms have conference facilities, and others are training rooms. Resources are things such as projectors, laptops, cameras, and so on. In one company I did training for, they had cars as resources!

There are two ways to select a room and resources. One is by clicking **Rooms**, which opens the Corporate Directory. We would do this if we need a particular room for our meeting such as a room that has conference facilities near our office or a training room. If we hold our cursor over each room while we have the Corporate Directory open, we can see the particulars of the room such as the number of people it can fit, whether it has conference or training facilities, and so on. Typically we would add the people we want to invite, then the particular room that we need, and we will then check the availability of both by using the scheduler.

The second way to select rooms is to use the **Find Rooms** button. I would always ensure the people I have invited are available via the scheduler and then use the **Find Rooms** button. This opens a dialog box. Many of the fields will be populated; check that these values are correct and then click the **Search** button. The search results will be displayed as a list below the **Search** button. Check to select the room returned in the search.

Reserving resources is basically the same except that we need to select the resource category, as resources are grouped under categories such as Laptops or Projectors.

We can set preferences so that we can have preferred rooms and resources and set our default site. This will be discussed further in this chapter.

The following is the search options' dialog box for Rooms:

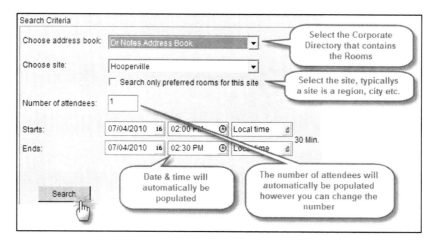

Finding available time with the scheduler

Using the scheduler when we are organizing meetings is very important. It is pointless to invite people to a meeting at a time when they are already booked! Using the scheduler allows us to see if they are available and, if we have been granted access to their calendar, we can actually see what they have going on.

We need to remember that if we grant someone access to our calendar, they can see all our calendar entries except the ones we **Mark Private**.

The scheduler can also give us suggested times if we are struggling to find a free slot. We can also deselect an individual if that person is too busy and see if everyone else is available.

The scheduler is a great tool and it should be used in every step of creating and updating meetings. When we create a meeting, we check everyone's availability, including rooms and resources if we have invited them. If we are rescheduling, we will see an option to **Check Schedules**; this will open up the scheduler to our proposed new time and we will be able to see everyone's availability. Even when we delegate, we need to check if the person we are delegating to attend the meeting is free. The scheduler will save time and assist us in being more efficient when managing meetings.

The **Find Available Times** scheduler has two sections — **Summary** and **Details**. Let's look at the Details first.

Scheduler: Details

The Details section shows time slots with color coding, showing the status of availability of each individual invited including rooms and resources. The colors are explained here:

- White (**Available**): This color indicates that the person is free.

- Red (**Already Scheduled**): This indicates the person already has something booked in their calendar at the time we are suggesting.

- Pink (**Unavailable**): This indicates that it falls outside of their normal working hours. These hours are set up in Calendar Preferences and will be discussed later in this chapter.

- Blue (**No Info**): This indicates the scheduler does not have any information regarding that person's availability. We will see this if we are inviting a person from outside of our organization.

- Gray (**Info Restricted**): This indicates the person we are inviting has chosen to not make their availability visible to us.

There is a difference between giving people access to see our availability and access to our calendar. If they can see our availability, all they see are blocks of when we are available or not available, and so on. If we give someone access to our calendar, they can double-click on the blocks, which in turn will open our calendar. By default, no one has access to our calendar and everyone has access to our availability via the scheduler.

The following is an example of the Scheduler. The bar shows the time block for the meeting. If it is green, it means everyone is available, whereas a red color indicates not everyone is available. The bar can be dragged to a different time slot or we can select a different date from the calendar and then double-click, and the bar will appear at the new date. We can also resize the bar to make the meeting shorter in time span or longer.

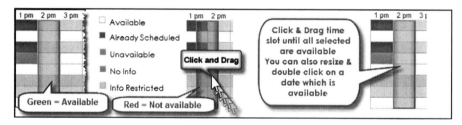

To check availability on a date not showing in the Scheduler, click the Calendar Picker, select a date, and then double-click on a time slot.

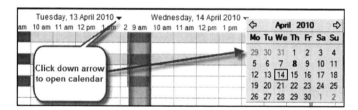

Finally, we can tweak who we invite. Each invitee will have a checkbox to the left of their name. If a person is very busy, we might want to consider deselecting his/her name and checking availability of all other invitees.

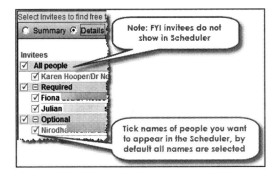

Scheduler: Summary section

The Summary section provides suggested times which we can select. Alternatively we can pick another date and see the suggested times for that date.

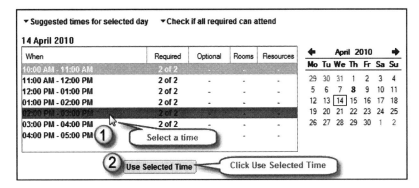

We can tweak the way the scheduler provides the suggested times as shown in the following screenshot:

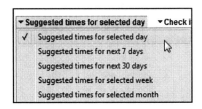

We can also change the way the scheduler checks for the attendees—for example, we can **Check if all required can attend** or **Check if at least 75% required can attend**, and so on.

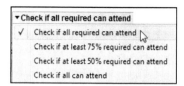

Managing meetings—be the chair!

When we create a meeting, we automatically become the chair. As the chair, there will be times when we need to check if people are attending, notify invitees, reschedule or cancel meetings. Managing meetings can be time-consuming, so take advantage of the tools we are going to see in this section to make that process more streamlined.

Checking if invitees are attending: View Invitee Status

It is important to know if our invitees are able to attend our meeting. We will have received their response in our inbox but sometimes we can miss these. I often view the responses from my invitees using the **View Invitee Status** and then use the **Print** button in that window and take the list to my meeting and use it as a sort of roll call. I believe there are two steps to a successful meeting—one is people responding to your invite, and second is their turning up!

There are a few ways to view the invitee status:

- From the calendar, select a meeting or open a meeting, click the **Owner Actions** button, and then select **View Invitee Status**. A window will open showing the responses from invitees; click the **Print** button if required.

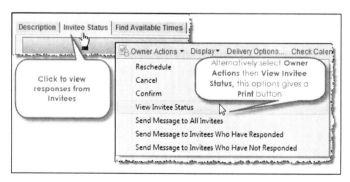

- Open a meeting and click the **Invitee Status** tab next to **Description** at the bottom of the document.

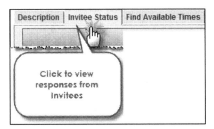

Sending a message to invitees

There are times when we need to send an e-mail to the attendees. We may have to remind them to bring their monthly reports, or we may want to inform them that lunch is provided. We can also send a message to those who have not responded and those who have, or just confirm the meeting.

From the **Owner Actions** button, there are several options to send a message to invitees.

We can:

- **Confirm**
- **Send Message to All Invitees**
- **Send Message to Invitees Who Have Responded**
- **Send Message to Invitees Who Have Not Responded**

Rescheduling meetings and cancelling meetings

As the chair we may need to reschedule a meeting due to changes in deadlines and at times even cancel meetings.

To reschedule a meeting, do any of the following:

- Drag-and-drop the meeting to another date on the calendar; the reschedule options will appear for us to update.
- Opening the meeting or selecting it from the calendar view, click the **Owner Actions** button and select **Reschedule**.
- Open the meeting and change the date or time.

If we are rescheduling, we will be prompted with **Reschedule Options**. These options allow us to select a new date and check the availability of invitees by clicking the **Check Schedules** button; there is no point in rescheduling a meeting when no one is available!

A reschedule notice will be sent to invitees. If rooms and resources have been booked, they will be rebooked for the new times if available. We should ensure without fail whether rooms and resources have responded with acceptances to our new times. It is a new low in life when we get rejected by a room, and even worse, when we turn up to our room for our meeting and find it occupied!

When we cancel a meeting, we can:

- Delete the meeting on our calendar
- Use the **Owner Actions** button and select **Cancel**

Depending on our preferences, the meeting will either be removed from our calendar or shown as cancelled. All attendees will be informed and their calendars will be updated. The cancellation process will also cancel the room and any resources booked.

Adding or removing additional invitees

Are our meetings so popular that when word gets out that we are having one, others want to come? Or one of our invitees has had a job change and he/she is no longer required in the meeting. Whatever is happening there may be occasions when we need to invite another person or remove an invitee after we have sent out the invitation. At any time we can open the meeting and add or remove invitees or additional rooms or resources. A meeting invitation will be sent to the new invitees only.

To add invitees, open the meeting and click on **Add Invitees**, whereas to remove, click on **Remove Invitees**.

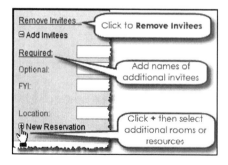

Calendar preferences

There are several calendar preferences that are excellent in helping us manage our calendar and our inbox. In preferences, we can select whether we see invitations on the calendar that as yet we haven't responded to (this is known as unprocessed meeting notices), we can also set up our hours of availability and delegate access to our calendar to name a few.

Calendar preferences can be accessed from within the calendar by clicking the **More** button and then selecting **Preferences** from the drop-down menu. We can also access calendar preferences via **File | Preferences | Calendar and To Do**. In this section, we will learn about some of the key areas in our calendar preferences.

Managing calendar notices (invites and responses) in mail

As we have mentioned, invitations to meetings come via the inbox as well responses to invites we have sent come into our inbox. There are preferences that we can set to manage the responses, which are known as notices.

1. In the **Calendar**, click on the **More** button and then select **Preferences**.
2. Select the **Notices** tab.
3. Select preferences for the **Calendar Notices in Mail Views** section.

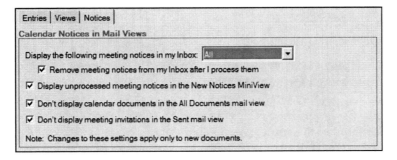

The choices available are:

- **Display the following meeting notices in my Inbox**: We can select to show none, or just invitations which is the choice **All except responses** (responses are replies to our meeting invitations such as acceptances, or **All**.)

- **Remove meeting notices from my Inbox after I process them**: This option is to remove meeting invitations once we have processed them, which is great as it keeps our inbox tidy. If we need to see the invitation, we can go to our **Calendar** and under **Views** select **Entries and Notices**. If it was an invitation we accepted, we will also see it as a meeting on our calendar. If we are a Smartphone user, this is also a great option as once we accept the meeting, the invitation is removed.

- **Display unprocessed meeting notices in the New Notices MiniView**: This is another great option. An unprocessed meeting is a meeting we have not responded to, that is, accepted or declined. We will cover this feature a bit later in this chapter as it is so good and highly recommended to be turned on. Here we are selecting to show unprocessed meetings in the MiniView; we will need to have the **New Notices** option selected to see the calendar entries as seen in the next screenshot:

- **Don't display calendar documents in the All Documents mail view**: All Documents is a fantastic view that contains all our e-mails that are in our Inbox, Sent folder, and our personal folders. It is a great place to search for e-mails. By default, calendar entries such as invitations, birthdays, and so on do not show in this view. Some people prefer to see only e-mails in this view and if they need to search for calendar entries in a view-like format, they go to the **Views** in the calendar.

- **Don't display meeting invitations in the Sent mail view**: When we **Save and Send** an invitation, we can select to have it displayed in the Sent folder.

Changes to these options are applied only to new documents created. So, if we enable any of these options after we have created calendar entries, we will still see them. We can remove them from the Sent mail view but not All Documents. To remove from the Sent mail view, select **Delete** and then select the option to **Remove**; be careful though, don't delete, only remove.

Automatic processing of invitations

We can set Lotus Notes to automatically respond to meeting invitations from anyone or a selected person or group of people. We may have a manger who requires our attendance at every meeting, so rather than manually accepting every invite, we can have Lotus Notes do it automatically for us. Follow the steps given here:

1. In the **Calendar**, click on the **More** button, then select **Preferences**.

2. Select the **Calendar & To Do** tab, and then the **Autoprocesing** tab.

   ° Select the **Respond automatically to meeting invitations** option

   ° Select who you want to automatically respond to

   ° Select acceptance actions

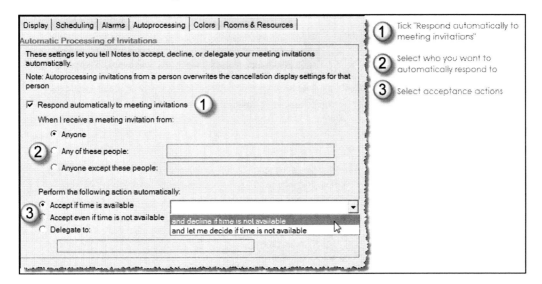

Setting our free time (availability) schedule

The term "Free Time" can be an oxymoron in our frantic world; however, in Lotus Notes free time represents the hours we are available to be booked for meetings. It is different than whether we have something booked in our calendar.

When people are checking our availability via the scheduler and we have something booked at the time, the timeslot they are looking at will be red. The pink color represents time outside of our available hours. White represents our time is available free time! To set the hours that we are available, we can open our calendar preferences and set days and times.

Be aware that people can still invite us to a meeting even if they see that we are either already booked or the time is outside of our available time. I know of some executives who, when setting up their availability schedule, deliberately made themselves not available for a time period in the afternoon. Their aim was to have a meeting free time so they could use that time to catch up. This area is great for part-time workers as we can give people an indication of what days we work.

Setting our available hours

Follow the steps given next:

1. From within our calendar, click **More** then **Preferences**.

2. Click the **Scheduling** tab.

3. Select the appropriate time zone from the **Time zone** list if necessary. Typically the default is **Local time**, which is our default time zone.

4. Select the days that we are available and the hours for each day on the **Scheduling** tab.

 We can copy and paste by highlighting text, selecting *Ctrl+C* and then *Ctrl+V* to paste to repeat day entries.

5. If we want Lotus Notes to prompt us if there is a conflict when we accept or create an entry, check the **Check for conflicts when adding calendar entries** option. This will prompt us when we have something already booked in our calendar.

6. The next option we can select is if we accept or create an entry that occurs outside our available hours. I never set this option as I know my hours and often I need to accept meetings outside of my availability. I really only want to be prompted when I have something actually booked in my calendar.

7. The last choice in this section is Inform **me when I send invitations to non-Notes users**.

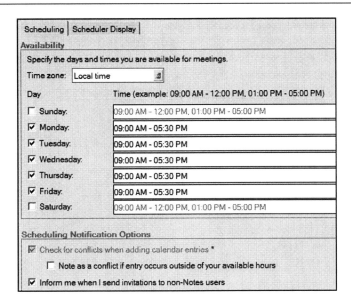

8. Click the **Scheduler Display** tab.

9. Select the display for when we are creating a meeting and referring to the Find Available Time section. We can set the default to be either Details or Summary, which is **Suggested best times for meeting**.

10. We can select if we want the scheduler to display in the 24-hour format.

Unprocessed and cancelled meeting preferences

Meeting invitations arrive in our inbox. In a busy inbox, we can accidently miss an invitation, a reschedule notification, or cancellation of a meeting. There is an excellent feature in our preferences where we can select to display invitations that we have not responded to in our Calendar and the Day-At-A-Glance. They will show in a gray color representing that we have not as yet "processed" the invite. All we need to do when we see one of these gray calendar entries is double-click to open and then either Accept, Decline, and so on. This saves us having to find the original invite in our mail. Having them grayed out on our calendar is similar to a mental note to prompt us to respond to the notice.

We can also set preferences as to how we want to process cancelled meetings. We can remove them from our calendar or **Show as cancelled in calendar**. I like the second option as often I like to check that the meeting was cancelled rather than realizing later that I have just missed it!

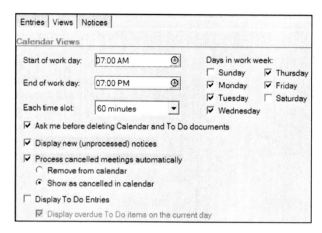

In this same area we can also select how we want our calendar to display, including the time of **Start of work day** and **End of work day**, plus time slot length and days in the **work week**.

Finally, we can decide how we want to display our To Do entries on our calendar. Check **Display To Do Entries** to see To Do on your calendar. Another option available is to **Display overdue To Do items on the current day**. If we select to show our To Dos on our calendar, be aware that they will follow us! If we have a To Do due today and we don't mark it as complete, it will be on our calendar until we mark it as complete. This can be a great tool to keep us aware of the To Dos that we need to complete; however, for some it can be overwhelming. Another option is to select to display our To Dos in the MiniView of our Calendar.

Default options

Within preferences, we can go to the **Display** tab and then the **Entries** tab. Here we can select default options for what entry type is created when we double-click on the calendar. We can also set the duration of meetings and appointments and how long our anniversaries repeat for. The default duration for meetings is 60 minutes; in the following screenshot I have changed the time to be **30 minutes**.

If we want to use categories within our calendar entries, set them on this tab as well as information for conference call information.

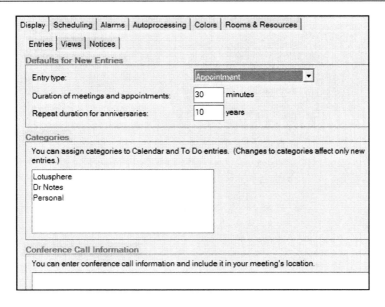

Alarms

I cannot live without alarms! In our calendar we can select to have alarms on by default for any of the different calendar entry types. We can also set the time. I turn my alarms on by default, and then when I create a calendar entry that doesn't need an alarm to be on, I turn it off for that entry. Many people work the other way and have alarms off by default and then turn them on for each individual entry. I highly recommend having alarms on for meetings, appointments, and reminders.

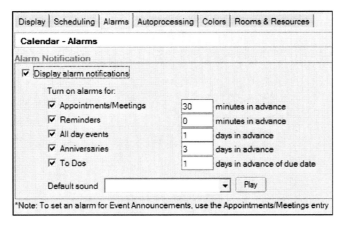

If we travel frequently, we can consider adding flight information and times as an appointment in our calendar. Set an alarm for one day prior on these appointments. When the alarm notifies us the day before we travel, we can use this as a trigger to do online check-in for our flight.

Colors

What is life without color! We can change the color coding for the different calendar entries in preferences. Simply go to the **Colors** tab and color away!

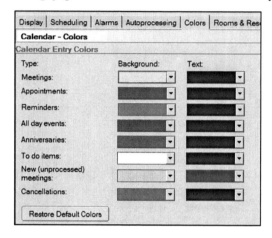

Delegating access to mail, calendar, To Do list, and contacts

It is often necessary for us to allow colleagues to have access to our mail or calendar. Assistants typically manager the e-mail and the calendar on behalf of their manager and therefore need a high level of access. Others just want work colleagues to see what they have booked in their calendar but not to see their mail. Granting access will be varied.

There are two types of access to our mail, calendar, To Do list, and contacts:

- **Via our schedule**: Typically everyone in the organization has access to our schedule. Our schedule shows our available hours and what times we have available. It does not show people the details of what we have booked in our calendar.

- **Via direct access to our mail/calendar/To Do/contacts**: Typically no one has access to our mail or calendar except to view our schedule. We can give someone direct access to our mail or calendar via preferences.

We can give another colleague access to our calendar as well as our mail, contacts, and To Dos. Follow the steps given next to give a person or group of people access.

1. Open **Mail** or **Calendar**, click the **More** button.

2. Select **Preferences**, and then **Access & Delegation**.

3. Select the **Access to Your Mail & Calendar** and then click the **Add** button.

4. Select the option to give access to **Everyone** or click the down arrow to open the address book to select name(s) or group(s).

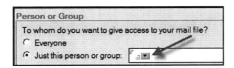

5. Select which components we want to give access to.

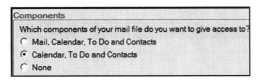

6. If we select **Mail, Calendar, To Do and Contacts**, the following options will be available to select. Read each level below to determine the appropriate level we want to apply to the person we have added. Notice that the fourth access level is the highest level of access.

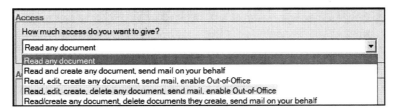

7. If we select the option of **Calendar, To Do and Contacts** (mail in this option is omitted), the following options will be available to select. Notice there are fewer choices available. Read each level to determine the appropriate level we want to apply to the person we have added.

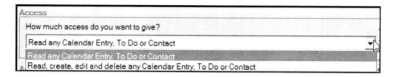

8. Finally, select any **Automatic Forwarding** options we require then the **OK** button.

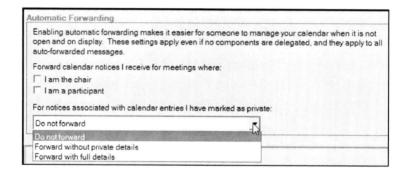

9. At any time we can **Remove** or **Change Access** to delegates we have added.

Setting defaults for room and resource reservations

When we book rooms or resources, we often book the same room/resource and we generally book them from the same site. In our calendar preferences, we can set a default site as well as favorite rooms and resources.

1. In the **Calendar**, click on the **More** button and then select **Preferences**.

2. Select the **Rooms & Resources** tab.

   ○ Click on the **Address Book** button to select **Preferred Site**. We can select if we want to use the site as a default and/or if we want to be prompted when scheduling within another site.

   ○ When we invite a new room in a meeting, we need to select if we want it to be added to the **Preferred Rooms** list. The available options are: **Always**, **Never**, and **Always ask**.

○ When we invite a new resource in a meeting, we need to select if we want it to be added to the Preferred Resources list. The available options are **Always, Never,** and **Always ask.**

○ Click the **Manage List...** buttons to add or remove rooms or resources.

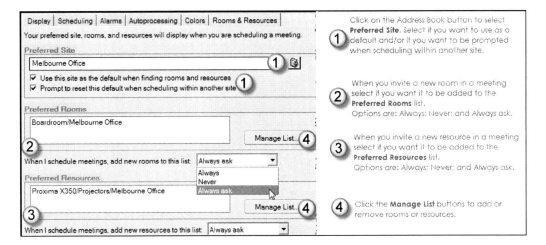

Rooms and resources

Rooms and resources are created and managed in the Resource and Reservations application. Typically only selected people and the IT Department have access to this application. When rooms or resources are created, there can be restrictions assigned to them such as only the owner can book the room or only specific people. If we book a room with owner restrictions, our booking will be pending until the owner approves or denies the booking. The following is the screenshot of the **Owner restrictions**:

Each resource can have a limit on the how far in advance a room or resource can be reserved.

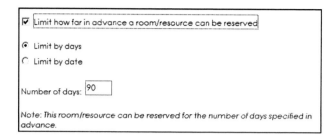

Automatic reminder notices for booked rooms

Automatic reminders can be enabled for all rooms and resources. Notices informing the chair of a meeting of the rooms they have booked can be sent out with an option for the chair to cancel according to when the reminder should be sent.

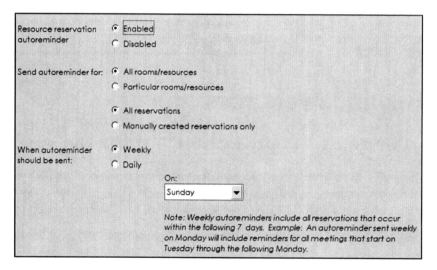

Printing the calendar

Even though we are living in the conceptual age of the "paperless office", we may still have to print our calendar every now and again. There are many options available for printing our calendar.

Open the print dialog box by having our calendar open and then selecting **File | Print** or *Ctrl+P*. The first tab we will explore is the **Printer** tab.

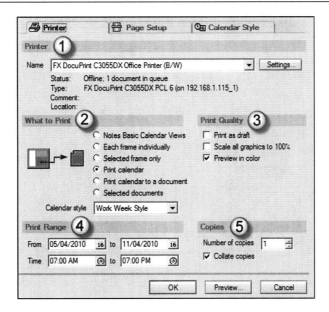

The **Print** dialog box has options on **What to Print** and **Print Range**. In the **What to Print** section there are some unique options; we can test them out by using the **Preview** button.

- **What to Print:** This is an area where we can determine how we want the print to be displayed. I recommend selecting each option and clicking the **Preview** button to view. As we select the different options, we will see the Page Setup and **Calendar style** tabs appear or disappear.

- **Print Range:** Depending on whether we are printing a month view or just one day, we can select the date range. The **Print Range** may not be available when we select some of the other **What to Print** options.

 I often use the **Print Calendar to a Document** option. This creates a Notes document, which I can not only print but also forward as an e-mail. Doing this, we can show someone our calendar without having to give them access.

The second tab is the **Page Setup** tab. On this tab we can select page margins, page orientation, and so on. Review the options below:

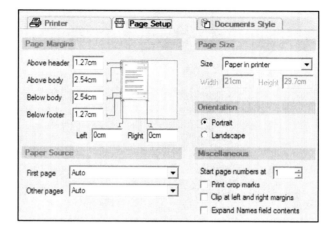

The last tab may or may not appear depending on what we have selected on the first tab in the section **What to Print**. If we have the option **Print Calendar** selected, the third tab is displayed as **Calendar Style** as shown in the next screenshot. Here we can select the fields that will be printed, whether we want to include weekends, and if we are printing so that we can add them to our Diary such as a DayRunner.

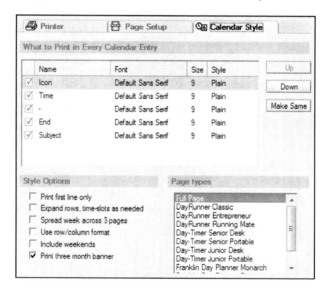

Calendar tools

Under the **More** button we can find some tools that are very useful. We have already discussed Preferences. In this section we will learn about importing holidays, opening other people's calendars, and calendar cleanup. We will discuss Group Calendars in another section.

Importing Holidays feature

Just the word "holidays" makes this feature sound great and it is indeed a great feature. Our IT Department can customize predefined holiday sets that are provided within Lotus Notes. We can then add them to our calendar. Holidays are typically categorized by country, although our IT Department could include regional holidays as well.

The following is the **Import Holidays** dialog box:

Each time we import, we will be prompted with what was added, updated, and what was deleted. At any time we want, we can import holidays and, if there have been any changes, these will be reflected in our calendar. We can also import another countries' holidays into our calendar. If we want to remove that country, we need to do the import, select our country only, and the additional country will be removed.

Opening another person's calendar

There may be times when we need to open one of our colleague's calendar. They must give us access before we are able to open their calendar. When we select **Open Person's Calendar**, we will be prompted with the Corporate Directory. We need to select the person's name then the **OK** button. That person's calendar will open so that we are able to view it.

If we need to access the person's calendar on a regular basis, we can create a bookmark to their calendar in our **Open** button. To bookmark, drag the window tab of the opened calendar to the **Open** button.

Calendar cleanup tool

Our calendars can be very busy and have lots of entries in them. We may want to cleanup old entries to reduce the space in our mail file or simply just tidy up. If we delete old entries, we run the risk of deleting future calendar entries if we have deleted a repeating appointment or anniversary, and so on. We can delete past calendar and To Do entries in a safe manner using the **Calendar Cleanup** tool.

To delete past calendar or To Do entries, we need to follow these steps:

1. Open the calendar or To Do.
2. Click **More** and then **Calendar Cleanup**.
3. Select which entries we want to delete by selecting **Entries older than** or **Entries occurring before**.
4. Select whether we want to delete **Calendar** and or **To Do** entries.

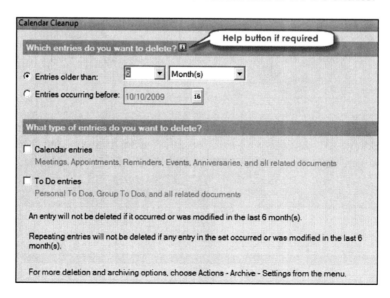

Managing imported calendars

We can import and export iCalendar-based calendars to and from Lotus Notes.

iCalendar is an Internet standard that allows calendars created in different calendar products to be imported into, and then viewed and managed in, other calendar products that use the iCalendar standard. The iCalendar standard also allows for the sending and receiving of meeting requests and other tasks via e-mail.

When a calendar is imported, the imported calendar entries are placed in the user's calendar and Lotus Notes creates an Imported Calendar document from which Notes users can manage the imported calendar. The Imported Calendar document contains the calendar name, a source field containing the path that specifies the location of the calendar file, and the date on which the calendar was imported into Notes. Imported calendar entries display in the user's Notes calendar as appointments, all-day events, anniversaries, or reminders.

From the Calendar Information document, users can manage their imported calendars in these ways:

- Delete a calendar using the Delete button
- Rename a calendar using the editable field

The Imported Calendar documents can be accessed through the Imported Calendars view. From this view, Notes users can view imported calendars, delete imported calendars, and import new calendars. To open the Imported Calendars view, we need to click **More** above the Notes calendar and then click **Manage Imported Calendars**. Notes users must upgrade their mail template to at least version 7.0.2 to use any of the new iCalendar import and export features.

If a user attempts to import a previously imported calendar, an information box indicates that the calendar already exists and asks whether to continue or cancel the import. The user can preview the calendar being imported prior to specifying whether to continue or cancel the import. If the user chooses to continue importing the calendar, the newly imported calendar overwrites the previously imported calendar.

Users can import iCalendar files with a maximum of 500 documents; multiple imports are required for more than 500 documents.

Notes also allows users to export their calendars by using **File | Export** to export all or selected calendar entries.

We can manage our imported calendars by following these steps:

1. Above the Notes calendar, we need to click the **More** button and then **Manage Imported Calendars**.

2. Do any of the following:

   ° To delete one or more calendars, select the calendars to delete, click **Delete**, and then click **Yes**.

   ° To edit a calendar's name, double-click the name of the calendar. Then click **Edit**, type a new calendar name, and click **OK**.

3. To import a new calendar, click **Import New Calendar**. Then select **Calendar File** (.ics) in the **Files of type** field, select the .ICS file to import, and click **Import**.

Overlaying another person's calendar

We can add many types of calendars to our Notes calendar, display their entries alongside our Notes calendar's entries (overlay them), and set display options to distinguish each calendar's entries from each other. I work with another trainer in my organization and I have overlaid their calendar onto mine so that when we are scheduling training I can see when we are either available or booked. I only tick to show my colleagues calendar when I am scheduling; all other times I have it deselected so that it doesn't show on my calendar.

1. In the **Views** panel of the calendar's navigator, expand **Show Calendars**.

2. Click **Add a Calendar**.

3. Under the **Add** drop-down box, select one of the options. Depending on the option we select, different fields will be required to be filed in. We then need to complete the **Add** fields for the **Add** option we selected.

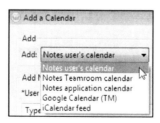

Let's now see each option under the **Add** drop down.

- ° **Notes user's calendar**: Adds another person's Notes calendar (requires that the person has given you access to their calendar). Type the person's name to search for them.

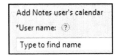

- ° **Notes Teamroom calendar**: Adds any Notes Teamroom that has a calendar. Enter the Label name (name of Teamroom) or URL into the appropriate fields and then click the **Lookup** button. A Teamroom application is used for teams to collaborate documents, calendars, and discussions.

- ° **Notes application calendar**: Adds any Notes application that has a calendar. We need to browse to the application and then select the application's calendar view. It is the same process as adding a TeamRoom calendar as above.

- ° **Google Calendar (TM):** Adds a private calendar (which requires a user name and password) or a public calendar (which requires the calendar's URL).

- ° **iCalendar feed**: Adds an iCalendar feed (requires the feed's Web address).

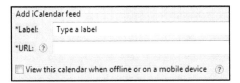

4. Under **Calendar Entry Formatting**, select display options to make the display of the added calendar's entries on your Notes calendar unique. Select background color, text color, and entry icon.

5. Click **OK**. If the calendar we're adding contains many entries, it may take a little longer for our Notes calendar to display them.

6. We can deselect to hide the calendar we just added and then select it again when we need it.

Group calendars

Group Calendars assist with managing several people's calendars in one location. They allow us to see everyone's availability in one window. If we have access to the members of the group calendar, we can also open their calendar. Group calendars are a great tool if we manage several people and need to view their availability and/or add and update entries in their calendars. For example, if we are a resource manager for consultants, we can add appointments for our consultants and view their availability within the group calendar.

Creating group calendars

1. Open the **Calendar** and expand the **Group Calendar** section on the side navigator.

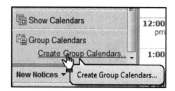

2. Click **Create Group Calendars** then click the **New Group Calendar** button.

3. Add a title and then add members by clicking the down arrow to select people from the address books. Then click the **OK** button.

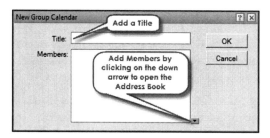

4. Once created, we can add members or remove members by clicking on the **Members** button in the group calendar.

5. Group calendars appear under the **Group Calendar** section.

6. When the group calendar is open, if we have access to any of the member's calendar, we can double-click their name and their calendar will appear in the bottom pane.

We can bookmark our favorite Group Calendar. We can do this by opening the Group Calendar and then dragging the window tab to the **Open** button.

Once opened, the group calendar is split into three areas. We have the members listed on the left-hand side, whereas their availability is listed on the right-hand side area. The bottom section is blank when we first open the calendar; however, if we double-click on a member's name, their calendar is opened in the bottom area (or preview area) as shown in the next screenshot:

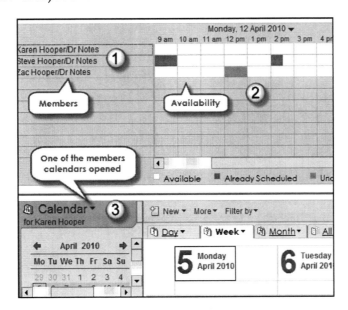

To Dos

To Dos are a fantastic tool in helping one organize his/her tasks. When we create our To Do, we can select a due date, priority, and whether the To Do should be assigned to us or to some other person. In preferences we can select whether or not we want to display our To Dos in our calendar. We can also display them in the MiniView.

As was shown with calendar and mail, there are different ways of opening To Dos.

To open To Dos, do one of the following:

- Click **Open** then select **To Do**.

- Select the **To Do** from the Home Page.

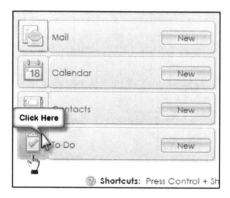

- From **Mail** or **Calendar**, we can switch to To Dos by clicking on the icon next to our name as shown here:

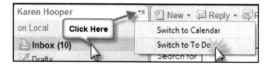

To Do side navigator

The To Do side navigator assists with managing our To Dos. The different views are described here:

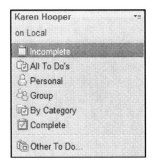

- **Incomplete**: For each To Do that we create, its status is incomplete until we click the **Mark Complete** button. We can also enter a **Due by** date. In this view we can see only To Dos that have the status of incomplete. The To Dos are categorized into **In Progress** and **Overdue** according to the **Due by** date.

- **All To Do's**: Contains all To Dos including completed ones.

- **Personal**: This view contains the To Dos that have been assigned to us. They are categorized by their priority—**High**, **Medium**, **Low**, and **Completed**.

- **Group**: As mentioned, we can assign To Dos to others. This view contains only those To Dos that have been assigned to others.

- **By Category**: Each To Do contains a **Category** field. If we have entered a value in this field, our To Dos will be organized under that **Category**. If we have left this field blank, they will be organized under **Not Categorized**.

- **Complete**: Contains all To Dos with the status of completed.

- **Other To Do**: We can open other people's To Dos. To do this we must go to preferences and set up **Shortcut to Others' Mail**.

 We can also see our To Dos in the MiniView by selecting To Dos from the drop-down list. The default for this area is typically **Follow Up**. We can also select to show To Dos on our calendar in our preferences.

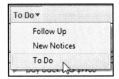

To Do action buttons

In each of the views that we described in the previous section, there are action buttons available. Their function is as follows:

- **New (1)**: Helps create new **To Do, Message, Contact, Group, Appointment,** and **Reminder**.

- **Mark Complete (2)**: This button changes the status to complete.

- **X (3)**: Click this button to delete the To Do.

- **Copy Into New (4)**: We have seen this button in both Mail and the Calendar. When we select a To Do and then this button, we have the choice to copy the information from the To Do into a **Message, Calendar Entry**, or another **To Do**.

- **More (5)**: In To Dos the submenu under the **More** button are **Preferences, Add Sender to Contacts,** and **Calendar Cleanup.**

- **Show (6)**: The Show button is available in Mail and Calendar as well as To Dos. This is where we can select to preview our To Dos.

Creating To Dos

When we create a To Do, we can put in as much or as little detail as we like, as there are no compulsory fields. Open **To Dos** and click the **New** button; this will open the **To Do** form. We need to fill in the fields as described below:

1. Select the **Priority**; the default is **Medium**. The other three choices are **High, Low,** and **None**.

2. Enter a short descriptive **Subject**.

3. Select the **Due by** and **Start by** dates. If we select a **Due by** date, many of the views will show if we are **In Progress** or **Overdue**.

4. Click the **Repeat** button if we required the To Do to repeat.

5. If this To Do is something for us to perform, leave the default value of **Assign to** as **Me**. If we want another person or a group of people to perform the To Do, select **Others** for the **Assign to** value and then enter their names into the **Required, Optional,** and **FYI** fields when they appear. These fields are hidden when the **Assign to** field has the value of **Me**.

6. Enter a value in the **Category** field. We can hide the **Category** field if we prefer by clicking the **Display** action button and deselecting **Display**.

7. Add further details into the **Description** area and an attachment if required by clicking the **Attach...** button. We can also drag-and-drop an attachment(s) into this area. Click the **Save and Close** button to save the To Do.

Another way to create To Dos is to use More...Copy Into New To Do. This is useful when we want to copy the information in the memo into the new To Do.

Assigning To Dos to others

The art of delegation is not lost with the ability to assign To Dos to others. Being able to delegate is great; however, one issue I have always found with delegating is the follow up. Asking someone to do something is quite simple, but for the delegation to be successful we need to know whether the person we have delegated to has completed the task.

This is where the To Dos in Lotus Notes excel. When we assign our To Do to others, they receive an invite to do the task. The following is an example of a To Do invitation. The red exclamation mark represents that the To Do is high priority. **Update CV** is the subject of the To Do and the date **12 Apr** is the Start date.

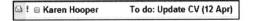

The process for assigning a To Do is very similar to when we invite someone to a meeting. When the assignee responds, they can **Accept**, **Decline**, **Propose New Date**, and **Delegate**. If accepted, the To Do will be added to the assignee's To Dos and we as the owner (person who assigned the To Do) will receive the response. For example, if the assignee accepted the To Do, it will appear accepted as in the following screenshot.

When the To Do is marked complete by the assignee, the owner is updated with a completed response as shown next:

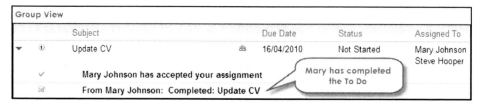

Once all assigned To Dos are complete, the owner can mark the To Do complete.

Marking To Dos complete

To mark a To Do complete, click the **Mark Complete** button in the view or from within the To Do.

Once we have marked a To Do complete, we can open the To Do in either the **Completed** view or the **All To Do's** view and **Mark Incomplete**.

We can set our calendar preferences to show To Dos on our calendar and we can set our MiniView to also show To Dos.

Summary

The calendar and To Dos are great tools for helping us manage our lives. Whether we use them for reminders and anniversaries or if we are a meeting junkie, the use of the Calendar and To Dos is invaluable.

In this chapter, we took a calendar tour, learned how to add entries to our calendar, and how to respond to and manage meetings. We explored calendar preferences and learned about Rooms and Resources as well as printing the calendar and using the different calendar tools. Finally, we explored group calendars and To Dos.

9

Working with Lotus Notes Applications

Lotus Notes is different from many other programs. It is an application that has many components, all wrapped into the one client. Some of the components of Lotus Notes such as Mail, Calendar, and Contacts have been covered in the earlier chapters of this book. A component we have not discussed in detail is Lotus Notes applications, also known as databases.

In this chapter, we will explore applications in Lotus Notes including:

- What is a Lotus Notes application
- Application examples
- Application templates
- Application security
- Printing

What is a Lotus Notes application

A Lotus Notes application is similar in concept and function to a Microsoft Access database just like Lotus Notes mail is similar to Microsoft Outlook and other mail systems such as Gmail.

An application or database is a container of data (hence the name database). Data can also be known as a record or in Lotus Notes language as a document. The documents within the Lotus Notes application can be displayed in various ways, manipulated by actions and workflow, and can store a variety of data such as text, rich text and files.

An application is made up of:

- **Forms**: An example of a form is the memo form in our mail. A form is a page with fields that we put values into such as the **To** field in the memo form. The following screenshot shows an example of a form in a timesheets application. We add times against a project that has tasks. The current **Workflow Status** of this timesheet is **Draft** as it is new.

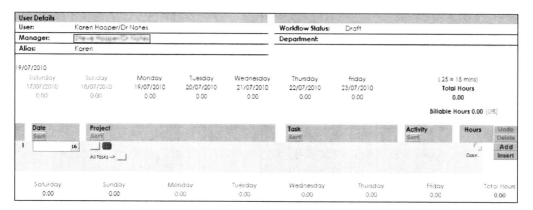

- **Fields**: We find fields in forms such as the **To** field in the memo example. Fields are where we enter data. Another example is our Contacts application. When we create a contact, we enter values into the **Name** field, the **Address** fields, and so on.

- **Documents**: When data has been entered into fields in a form and it is saved, it becomes a document. In other database systems, a document may be referred to as a record.

- **Views**: Store and display documents in columns and can be categorized. For example when we were learning about To Dos, we discussed a view called **Complete**. This view showed only To Dos where the **Status** field had the value of complete. In another view called **Incomplete**, we saw only documents (or To Dos) that did not have the value of complete. In the **All To Dos** view, we can see all To Dos. We can have three different views in an application that show different documents depending on how the views were designed. The columns in views display the fields in the forms. For example, in the All Documents view in our mail, the **Subject** column displays the **Subject** field in the memo. The following screenshot is an example of views available in a timesheets application. To see timesheets in progress, we would select the **In Progress** view, or if we were an approver of timesheets, we would go to the **Ready For Approval** view.

- **Folders**: Folders are designed for the users of the application to be able to add documents to them. Using the mail example again, we can create folders to file messages in.

- **Actions**: Actions are available in the form of buttons, in a form or document and in views Actions may also be accessed via the menus. Actions, as the name implies, when clicked or selected from a menu, perform an action. A very common action is a **Save and Close** button in a form. An example of an action in an e-mail is the **Send** button. The following screenshot shows an action button from a timesheets application. Once a person has added their times into the timesheets form, they would click the **Submit for Approval** button to submit it to their manager for approval, which is part of the workflow cycle.

- **Access Control List**: This is also known as ACL. The access control list is all about security. It has a list of people's names or groups with different levels of access to the application. The different levels are:

    ○ **Manager**: This is like the owner of the application. As a manager one can edit the access control list and add, rename, and remove members. We can also change the level of access for members. A manager can also delete the application. This is the highest level of access and it incorporates all the other access levels.

    ○ **Designer**: As the name implies a person with this level of access can make design changes to the application. If a new view is required a person with designer access would be able to create that new view.

    ○ **Editor**: With this level of access we can typically create and edit any document within the application.

    ○ **Author**: An author can create documents but can only edit the documents that they create.

        °   **Reader**: Can only read documents.

        °   **Depositor**: This role can only add documents. This level of access is used for applications designed for voting or questionnaires, and so on. In such applications, we just enter our information—for example, we submit the form and can't read anyone else's information, or our own information once submitted.

The following is an example of an Access Control List. The highlighted area in the right-hand corner is the available levels of access.

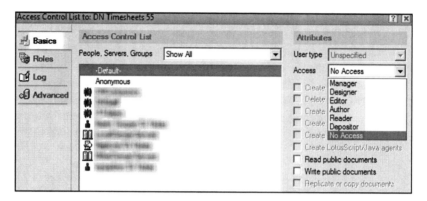

An application is one file with a file extension of `.nsf`. Lotus Notes applications are stored in the data directory of the Lotus Notes program by default; however, they can be placed in other locations, and whoever installs the application can determine the location. Lotus Notes applications are normally stored on servers, and hence it is known as client/server software.

An example of an application stored on a server (known in Lotus Notes as a Domino server) is mail. The mail application resides on the server but can also reside on the client in the local PC's data directory. The benefit of having the mail in the two locations is that it can be accessed when there is no connection available to the server, for example, if one is at 36,000 feet up in the air in a plane!

There are two different types of applications within Lotus Notes—ones that are stored only on your PC or laptop and those that are shared. The shared applications must reside on a server. The shared application can also reside on our PC or laptop via a special copy called a replica.

The shared application can reside on one server or several servers. This enables collaboration for users on each of the servers, which are typically in different locations. For example, we may work for an international organization and have an office in Melbourne, Australia and another in New York, U.S.A. Both countries would be able to share the information stored in the Lotus Notes application and, if they have the correct level of access, they may be able to add and edit the information stored. Often, when we want to share information we add an attachment and e-mail it. Many times files are stored on network drives, which are typically only accessible locally. Within Lotus Notes we can create documents to store information and attachments. As Lotus Notes applications can be accessed by many people at the same time and can be replicated to servers all over the world, the benefit of storing the files within a Lotus Notes application is invaluable.

An example of an application that would reside only on our PC or laptop would be the Notebook application. The Notebook as its name implies, is a place to add notes similar to a journal; in fact in an earlier version of Lotus Notes it was called a Journal. An example of a shared application is the Corporate Directory, which everyone has access to as it resides on the Domino servers.

Most Lotus Notes applications are created from templates. Lotus Notes templates have a file extension of .ntf. For example, when the Notebook application is created, it is created from the notebook8.ntf template. Locally (which means on your PC or laptop) there are quite a few templates that have been installed when Lotus Notes was installed. We will explore some of these templates in this chapter.

Companies can also create and customize their own Lotus Notes applications. For example, companies may have applications for tracking expenses, artwork approval, leave approval, asset management, or they might use Lotus Notes for discussion forums such as blogs or community bulletins. A Lotus Notes application can be very simple and also very complex depending on the functionality and purpose.

The great benefit that Lotus Notes gives is that the interface and the actions we do within the applications are similar across all components of Lotus Notes including mail, contacts, and applications. Also because it is all within the one client, we don't have to have several applications running; all we need is Lotus Notes!

Application examples

Lotus Notes applications can be customized to suit just about any type of situation. There is a programming layer built into Lotus Notes, which enables applications to be developed in very efficient and cost effective time frames. Because there is a mail component within Lotus Notes, workflow can be built into the applications with ease. The following are examples of some of the applications I have seen built with Lotus Notes. These applications would be accessed on a server or servers (shared):

- **SOP Application (Standard Operation Procedures)**: I have seen this application many times. The design within the different organizations has been varied. Some companies enter the SOPs directly into documents in the application. Others have created their SOPs in Microsoft Word or Symphony and have then put each SOP file as an attachment into its own document in the application. Most applications I have seen have had an approval workflow.

- **CRM (Customer Relationship Management)**: This application typically contains client information and contact details.

- **Project Management Application**: Managing projects is a time-consuming task. I have seen Lotus Notes applications that have been built to assist in managing this process. The applications have forms where we can enter the details of each project such as customer/client, times frames, the team working on the project, and any tasks involved. Some organizations may have a timesheet application that is incorporated with the project management application. When timesheets are submitted, the times are put against the projects so that those responsible can see if they are on track or running overtime.

- **Timesheets Application**: At Dr Notes, the company I work for, we are predominately a services and training company and hence most of our employees are consultants. As consultants we go out on site to customers or support them remotely. When we do this we need to track our time. In the timesheets application we have a document for each week. We enter our time against the different projects we have running. We then submit our timesheets at the end of each week. Our manager is automatically notified by e-mail that we have submitted our timesheets. Within the e-mail they receive there is a link to each of our timesheets, which they can click on and approve. If approved, our times are sent to the Project Management application to be put against the appropriate project. From there the information is sent to our financial system, which then uses the data for billing purposes. These steps are generally known as workflow. Many organizations that build similar Lotus Notes applications will create their own workflows for each application they build.

The applications discussed in the above bullet list were all customized for each organization. We can also create an application from the standard templates that are provided with Lotus Notes. To create an application from a template is very quick and easy as the template has prebuilt forms, views, and so on. Each template has an About document that describes its purpose; I have quoted from the About documents so as to give an accurate description for each template described below:

Examples of standard template applications

The following list shows examples of standard application templates:

- **Teamroom Application**: This application is great for information sharing and collaboration. It is designed to enable teams to:
    - Raise and discuss issues and concerns.
    - Create memos, presentations, and other "deliverables" within the application.
    - Brainstorm (which hopefully leads to resolution and action).
    - Prepare oneself for presenting and sharing information in the TeamRoom before the meeting so that meeting time can be focused on decision making.
    - Track meeting agendas and resulting action items.

- **Discussion Application**: A workgroup can use this application to share their thoughts and ideas. Almost any group that has information to share among its members can use a discussion application. An engineering group can discuss the products they are designing. An advertising agency can discuss the ad campaigns they are developing. A special interest group can share ideas and opinions on their common interests.
    - To get started, a user can simply browse through discussion topics and responses that others have contributed. This is particularly useful for new workgroup members who need to come up to speed on important issues that the group is working on. The history of discussion about these issues is preserved in the group's discussion application.
    - A user can also take a more active role in the discussion by composing their own responses to others' comments and by proposing new main topics for discussion.

- A discussion application is an informal meeting place, where the members of a workgroup can share ideas and comments. Like a physical meeting, each member of the workgroup listens to what others have to say and can voice their own opinions. However, unlike a physical meeting, the participants do not have to be in the same room at the same time to share information. People can participate when it is convenient for them to do so, and because it is easy for them to share information, they will do so.

- **Blog**: This application allows us to create individual or team-based "blog" websites or other types of content-based websites. The application works straight out of the box after completing a simple creation wizard. Current features of this application are:

    - Template and tag-based design makes it easy to change default designs to suit individual or corporate requirements.
    - Full built-in RSS feeds from content/comments and categories of content.
    - Comment/discussion system with anti-spam functionality.
    - Future automatic publishing or expiry of content.
    - Notes and web-based content editing.
    - Supports podcasting, automatic content archiving and searching, and social bookmarking.

- **Document Library**: A document library application is an electronic filing cabinet that stores reference documents for access by a workgroup. The application might contain anything from environmental impact statements for a group of engineers to financial statements for a group of loan officers.

- **Microsoft Office Library**: This application gives Notes users the ability to seamlessly create and save documents using Microsoft Word, Excel, PowerPoint, or Paintbrush, without leaving Notes. In addition, the library serves as an electronic filing cabinet for these documents, making it easy for all members of a workgroup to locate, update, and print desired documents. The application might contain anything from environmental impact statements for a group of engineers using Word to financial statements for a group of loan officers using Excel. Besides being a repository and point of interaction for documents created with Microsoft application software, the document library includes other important document management features. These features include archiving and review cycle capabilities.

Local (PC or laptop) applications

We can create an application from a template on our local PC. An example of one available template is the Notebook, which is described below. On the Homepage there is a button to access the Notebook. If we have not created one, it will create one on our behalf. If we want to create another Notebook application, go through the *Creating an application from a template* section.

The Notebook application is designed to keep private documents and is not intended to be shared with others. We can use our Notebook as a diary, to store meeting minutes or status reports, or simply as a place to create and store draft documents until they are ready for publication. We can create, categorize, and print Notebook entries.

Template and application information

Standard Lotus Notes applications will usually have an About document. This document describes the purpose of the application.

To access the About document for templates, we need to follow the steps given next:

1. Select **File | Application | New**. The **New Application** dialog box opens.
2. Under **Specify Template for New Application**, select the server the template resides on.
3. Select the template we want to know more about. Click on the **About** button on the right-hand side. This will open a document describing the application purpose.
4. Click **Cancel** to close the **New Application** dialog box.

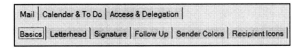

If we have created an application or we are accessing, we can access the **About** document. We can also view the **Using** document that describes how to use the document by doing the following:

1. Open the application.
2. Go to the **Help** menu, select **About this Application**, press the *Esc* key to close the document.
3. If we want to know how to use the application, we need to select **Using This Application** from the **Help** menu.

4. Press the *Esc* key to close the **Using this Application** document.

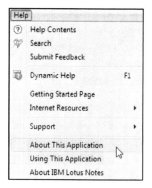

Creating an application from a template

We need to follow the steps given next to create an application on our local PC or laptop from a template:

1. Select **File | Application | New**, the **New Application** dialog box will open.

2. In the **Server** field, leave the value of **Local**. This means that the application we are creating will be saved onto our local PC or laptop.

3. Enter a **Title** for the application.

4. The **File Name** will be automatically filled in from the title of the application. We can change the filename if desired. The application will be saved into the Lotus Notes data directory; to change this click the folder button.

5. By default the application will be encrypted with our ID, which means only our ID will be able to open it. This is a security measure and is highly recommended. To remove encryption, click the **Encryption** button and select **Do Not Locally Encrypt this database**.

6. Check the **Create a full text index for searching** option. If the application has an index, searching is very fast and we can search for words within documents using wildcards, and so on.

7. We now have to select the template. We have to leave the default value of **Local** for **Server** if the template we want to create from is on our PC or laptop. If the template is on a server, select r4t server.

8. Select the template. If we want to know about the template, click on the **About** button to the right-hand side. This will open a document describing the application purpose.

9. Click the **OK** button to create the application.

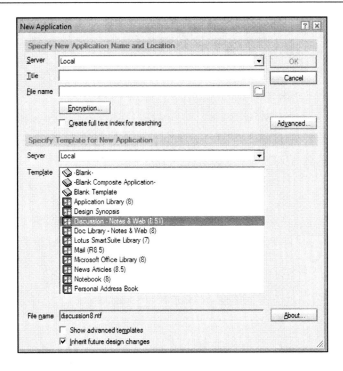

Application properties

Each application has properties. The properties give us information on the following:

- Title of an application.
- The location of the application, including which server it resides on and the path of its file.

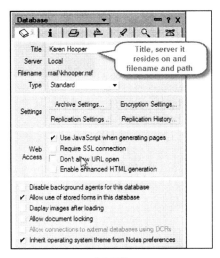

- The size of database and how many documents it contains.

- It also gives us assist us with when we need to compact our application. The % used button will show how efficiently the space available in the application is being used. Compacting improves the efficiency by removing white space created when we delete documents.

- Clicking on the **Compact** button deletes white space left after deleting documents.

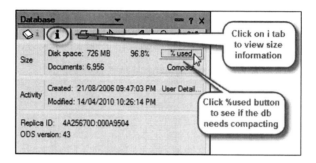

Changing application security

Each application has an Access Control List (ACL). We discussed the ACL earlier in this chapter as it is the security component of a Lotus Notes application. When we create an application, we automatically become the manager, which means we have the highest access. Only a manager is able to add, remove, or change the access of people listed in the ACL.

We can access the ACL by opening the application and then selecting **File | Application | Access Control...**.

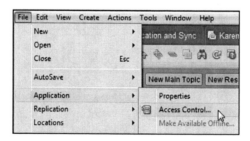

To add a person to the ACL, click the **Add...** button and select their name from the Corporate Directory. Assign a level of access. To change the level of access for a person, select the person's name and then assign the new level of access. To remove a person from the ACL, click the person's name and then the **Remove** button.

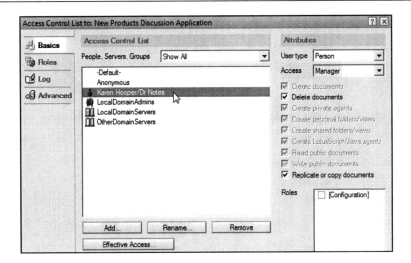

Opening applications

To open an application, go to **File | Open | Lotus Notes Application** or *Ctrl+O*. Select the server the application is located on; leave the **Look in** field as **On my Computer** if the application is on our PC or laptop.

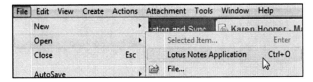

We can perform any of the following tasks with the application:

- **Open**: Opens the application.
- **Cancel**: Closes the **Open Application** dialog box.
- **Bookmark...**: This button allows us to save an application to the Open List or the Bookmark Bar. This is explained in later sections.
- **About ...**: Opens the About document which describes the application.

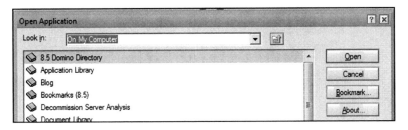

Bookmarking an application

When we are opening an application, we have the opportunity to bookmark the application so that we can easily access it again. When we click the **Bookmark...** button in the **Open Application** dialog box, we get the following options:

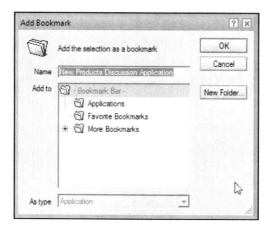

If we select **OK**, the application will be added to the **Bookmark Bar**, or **Open** list. If we want to add the application to an already existing folder such as the **Applications** folder, click the folder and then the **OK** button. To add a new folder, click the **New Folder** button.

In the next screenshot, I have added the **New Products Discussion Application** to the **Open** list.

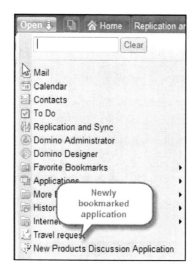

If we have the application open, we can drag the window tab to the **Open** list to bookmark it. We can also right-click the Window tab when we have the application open and select **Bookmark**....

The following is a description of the different folders available in the **Open** list. When we open applications, we can add applications to these folders.

Folder	Description
	The Favorite Bookmarks folder gives us a place to store our favorite or most often-used bookmarks.
	The Applications folder: If we upgrade from an earlier release of Lotus Notes that did not have bookmarks, Lotus Notes automatically puts copies of all our workspace icons into the Applications folder. The workspace pages appear as folders, and the workspace icons appear as bookmarks inside those folders. We can access our Workspace from this bookmark folder.
	The More Bookmarks folder contains a Lotus Links folder, the Internet Search Sites folder, and a Create folder.
	The History folder keeps a chronological listing of bookmarks for all documents, views, applications, and web pages we visit during the course of a day, with the most current item at the top of the list. Dated subfolders within the History folder contain the bookmark lists from the last seven days.
	The Internet Explorer Links contains links we have created with these browsers.

Links

In Lotus Notes we can create hyperlinks or shortcuts to applications, views, folders, and documents. There are times when someone may send us a link to an application they want us to access. We simply click on the link and the application will open. While it is open, we can bookmark it if we need to access it again.

We can also create links to views and documents. If there is a particular view or document in a view that we want someone to look at, we can create a link and send it to them.

Creating a link to a document, view, folder, or application

We need to follow the instructions given here to create links:

1. Open the document, view, folder, or application we want to create a link to.

2. Select **Edit | Copy As**, and then select the type of link. We can select from **Table, Anchor Link, Document Link, View Link**, and **Application Link**.

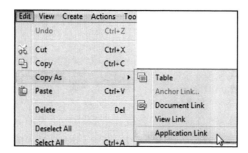

- ○ **Table**: Creates a table with rows and columns.

- ○ **Anchor Link…:** This adds an anchor link icon next to a paragraph.

- ○ **Document Link**: We will need to have a document open or have a document selected that we want to create a link to. When the link is clicked, the document will be opened.

- ○ **View Link**: This time we will need to be in a view or folder. When the link we created is clicked, the view or folder will be opened.

- ○ **Application Link**: Open the application we want to create a link to. When this link is clicked, the application will be opened.

3. Put the document that we are adding the link to in edit mode. This can be done by opening it and then double-clicking or clicking the **Edit** button if one is available. Note that when we create an e-mail it is in Edit mode. When we read an e-mail it is in Read mode.

4. Click where we want the link to appear.

5. Select **Edit | Paste** or *Ctrl+V*.

6. Click the link to test.

If we are creating a link to an application and we are going to send that link to another person, make sure that person has access to the application before we send the link.

Copying a view and pasting it as a table

We can copy any application view and then paste the view to appear as a table in a document or into a spreadsheet and so on. When we paste the view into a document, the column titles in the table match the column titles in the view and the first column gives us a doclink to each document listed in the table. When we click on the doclink, it will launch another tab and open the corresponding document.

The rows in the table match the documents selected in the view that was copied. To create the table, select the documents, click **Edit | Copy As | Table** and then paste into desired location.

The following is an example of a pasted view:

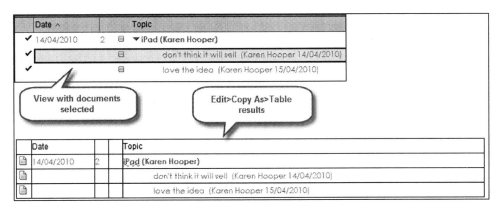

Summary

Lotus Notes is a fantastic application solution if an organization has invested in Lotus Notes. Applications can be purchased off the shelf, they can also be custom built, or they can created from the templates available.

Learning how to use each application is simplified as they have a similar interface to Mail, Calendar, and Contacts.

In this chapter we have explored the different aspects of the Lotus Notes application including examples and how to create your own!

10
Working Remotely (Replication/Synchronization)

Recently the White House hosted a forum on workplace flexibility where the benefits of working remotely were discussed. To quote Joe Davidson from the *Washington Post*:

> *Obama was speaking at a White House forum on workplace flexibility Wednesday and used the days that snow forced federal offices in Washington to close as an example of why the public and private sectors should adopt some alternative arrangements, such as telework, for their employees.*

Telework is to work from home or outside the traditional office or workplace, using a computer or telephone connection.

Working away from the office is a popular alternative in this day and age, and often a more economical and greener alternative for organizations. No longer are we office bound as many of us have the flexibility and the technology available to work away from the office.

Working remotely for us could be that our workplace is our home. For others their job may call for them to travel, the office for them could be airports or hotels. Whatever our work situation, being able to work remotely is an important tool and many companies have formal remote-working policies in place as well as the infrastructure to facilitate them.

In this chapter we explore how to work remotely using Lotus Notes.

Working offline in Lotus Notes

There are several components that enable us to work remotely in Lotus Notes. We will cover the steps to incorporate these components in this chapter.

Replica

A **replica** is a special copy of a Lotus Notes application that synchronizes with another replica, exchanging data so that they become the same. When we access our mail at the office, we typically open our mail on a server. To work offline we need to create a copy of our mail locally on our computer. That copy needs to be able to synchronize so that any mail that we received at the office can be copied to our mail on our computer and any messages that we have sent or filed locally are copied back to our mail on the server.

In Lotus Notes this copy is called a replica because it has the ability to synchronize documents between other Notes applications—sending documents to other replicas and receiving from other replicas. To create the replica, we need to open the application on the server such as our mail and select the **Make Available Offline** option (there are step by step instructions later in this chapter).

Replication (Synchronize)

Replication is the process of synchronizing documents and updates between replica applications. When replication (also known as synchronization) occurs between two replicas, documents and changes are compared in each replica. If a new document such as an e-mail message is in one replica and not the other, the replicator will create it in the latter. The replicator's job is to send and receive any changes that have been made so that both replicas are the same. To use mail as an example, changes could be a new message, a newly created folder, filing of messages, or a repeating calendar entry being changed.

The following is a diagram of an example of replication. Bob has a replica of his mail on the organizations server and another on his laptop. Currently in the example shown next, the replica on the server has different documents than the one on Bob's laptop. Bob may have been away from the office for a period of time and he may have created some new messages, but as yet has not connected into the office to replicate.

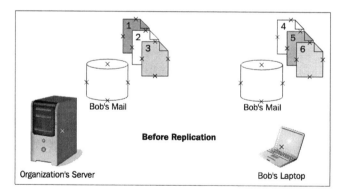

In the next diagram Bob has connected into the office and replication is in progress. The arrows represent the sending and receiving of documents.

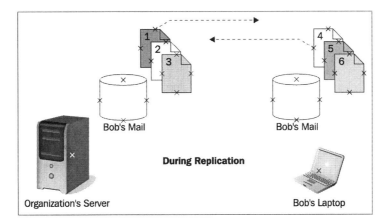

In the final diagram we can see that the documents in Bob's mail on the organization's server and the documents in Bob's mail on his laptop as the same. This is because they have been synchronized via the process of replication.

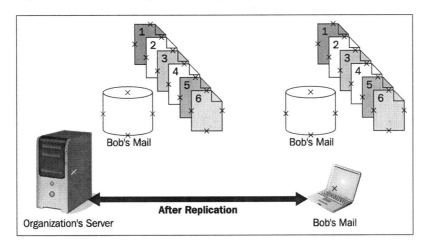

Replication and Sync page

This is a special place in Lotus Notes that is designed to assist with managing replication, this is the Replication and Sync page. It lists the replicas on our computer, includes buttons to start and stop replication, and shows how many documents were sent and received. When we start replication, it will show the progress of replication for each replica. We can manually replicate from this page or create a schedule to replicate according to a timeframe.

The following is an example of the **Replication and Sync** page:

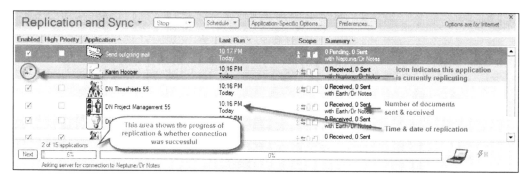

Locations

When we start Lotus Notes, we may be asked to select our location; alternatively we can select our location from the password prompt dialog box or in the locations area in the status bar. Locations tell Lotus Notes where to access applications. For example, when we are using the **Online** location, we are typically connected to Domino servers via the network. This means we are getting the latest e-mails and updates to applications continuously. When we are using the **Offline** location, Lotus Notes knows to access the mail replica on our computer rather than the server as **Offline**, means we have no connection to any network or Domino server.

Online (previously known as Office) means we are in the office, connected, and we are using one of the following:

- Docking station
- Wirelessly
- Via a network cable
- Via VPN remotely

Offline (or also know as Island) means we are *not* connected — for example, we may be in a plane, in a hotel without an Internet connection, or a tropical island without Internet connection (we wish!), and so on.

 The **Home** and **Travel** location documents are no longer used but remain for backward compatibility reasons.

When I am travelling and on long flights, I take advantage of that time and tidy up my mail. It is a great time to file e-mails, sort out folders, and delete unwanted e-mails. When I am in the plane, I select the **Offline** location.

To view location documents, we need to select **File | Locations | Manage Locations**. We can also access locations via **File | Preferences** and then select **Locations**. From within this area, we can create new location documents as well as edit, copy, or delete location documents, we discuss this later in the chapter.

We can see our current location in the status bar as shown here:

Connection documents

Connection documents tell Lotus Notes how to connect to servers. We have mentioned that our mail is on a mail server. Applications that are shared reside on a Domino server. To replicate our mail and applications, we will need to be able to connect to the server that they are located on.

A connection document contains information Lotus Notes needs to connect to a Domino server. It contains the Domino server's name and network address. We can view connection documents by opening our contacts and clicking **View | Advanced | Connections**.

We may already have the connection documents that we need to access Domino servers when we are connecting remotely. To create a connection document, we need to switch to the relevant location document and then select **Tools | Client Reconfiguration Wizard** and enter the details required.

To get to our mail server within our organization, we may have to pass through another server. To do this we will need a pass-through connection document that will include the details of the pass-through server. We will then need a connection document to the server where our mail is located, which is known as your home server. This can sound complicated, however, it is quite simple and most often this is already set up for us by our IT Department. In some organizations, connection documents may not be necessary as the organization is accessed via VPN (Virtual Private Network) or RAS (Remote Access Service) and the **Online** location.

ID file

When we start Lotus Notes, we will likely be prompted for our password. Our password is stored in our ID file. If we are prompted for our password, we will need to ensure that our ID file is available on our computer. The ID file typically has a file extension of .id. We can perform a search on our computer by searching for *.id. Be aware that copies of our ID file can have different passwords. We need to test if we can start Lotus Notes while disconnected and that we know the password.

Mobile directory

This is a special copy of the Corporate Directory that contains all the personnel within our organization. If we have the mobile directory available to us on our PC when we are sending a message, we will be able to look for names in our Contacts and the Corporate Directory. If we do not have a Mobile Directory, then we will not be able to see the Corporate Directory only our Contacts. It may have a different name such as Mobile Directory or DirCat. It is special because it is lightweight in size and typically quick to replicate. It does not contain all the details that the Corporate Directory does, such as group membership, as this is how it remains lightweight.

Outgoing mail application

We can send messages while we are disconnected and they will be sent from mail to our Outgoing Mail application. The Outgoing Mail application is where mail is stored until Lotus Notes can establish a connection to the Domino mail server. To send mail from the Outgoing Mail application, we will need to be connected. The Outgoing Mail application is created the first time we switch from the **Online** location to any of the offline locations available.

When we replicate, it will send any e-mails pending in the Outgoing Mail application. If we have been offline and we have sent e-mails then, when we come into the office and switch to the **Online** location, Lotus Notes will prompt us with saying how many messages are pending and if we want to send them.

We typically do not need to open the **Outgoing Mail application**, but if you do, then we need to go to the **Replication and Sync Page** and double-click on **Send outgoing mail.**

This is the opened Outgoing Mail application.

 We can open the Outgoing Mail application and delete a message that we accidently sent if we have not as of yet replicated. We need to be aware that the message will still appear in our Sent mail; we can delete it from here as well if we wish. If we have Message Recall enabled in our organization, we could use that as well.

Preparing to work remotely

In this section we will explore the steps we need to complete to enable us to use Lotus Notes when we are disconnected or away from the office. There are a varied number of ways that we may connect into our organization remotely. How we connect will not be covered in this chapter and it will be presumed that we can connect.

In some organizations these steps have been completed by the IT Department before we are given our laptop. However, it is recommended to still go through the steps so that we are confident to work remotely.

Step 1: Setting up applications:

We need to set up applications so that they can be accessed locally. We need to follow these steps before we leave the office:

1. Create local replicas of our mail and any other applications that we will need to access offline. We discuss how to do this later in the chapter. If our mail or any application is large in size, creating the replica could take a while. We can create the replica in the background so that we can continue working. Just don't try and create the local replicas five minutes before you leave the office!

2. Test accessing our local replicas when disconnected, by unplugging the network cable or disabling wireless. Make sure we remember to reconnect our network.

3. If we are prompted to enter a password when we start Lotus Notes, we will need to make sure our ID file is on our computer. To test, once we have disconnected from the network in the preceding step, restart Lotus Notes. It will prompt us if it can't find our ID.

4. We need to discuss with our IT Department if we need to create any connection documents to access our home server.

5. We need to ensure our remote access is set up and ready to go. Discuss this with the IT Department and make sure we have all the software and login details, including passwords that we require to connect when we are away from the office.

Step 2: Testing remote access from home

We need to follow these steps to test remote access from home:

1. Start up the laptop and ensure you are not connected to the office.

2. Start up Lotus Notes, select the **Offline** location. Test opening mail and any applications that have local replicas.

3. Create and send a message.

4. Go to the **Replication and Sync** page and open the Outgoing Mail Application by double-clicking **Send Outgoing Mail**. Once opened we should see the message that we just sent.

5. Connect into our organization.

6. Open the **Replication and Sync** page and click the **Send** button. Leave the **Replication and Sync** page open and watch to see if the message was sent. We can open the Outgoing Mail application to confirm that it is empty.

Step 3: Setting up a schedule

If required we can set a schedule to enable replication to occur according to a set timeframe. This is done by clicking the **Schedule** button on the **Replication and Sync page**.

In some organizations, it is recommended not to change location documents and to stay on the Online location when we connect in remotely, by VPN or RAS for example.

When we change to the other locations, we access our mail locally on our PC. When we open a large attachment in our local replica, we are doing it locally on our PC. When we open a large attachment when using the **Online** location, we are opening it over the network at the server. This can be slower than working locally.

Also there may be times when we cannot connect into the office because the connection could be intermittent or we're in a no network area. When this occurs, we will not be able to access mail or any of our other applications if we do not have local replicas. I like the flexibility and speed of working locally. I only work **Online** when I am at the office.

Next we look at how to take our applications offline by creating local replicas.

Enabling an application to be accessible offline (Creating Local Replicas)

To be able to access applications when we are away from the office, we will need to create a local replica. We need to follow the steps given next to allow our applications to be accessed when we are away from the office.

1. Open the application we want to take offline.

2. Select **File | Application | Make Available Offline**.

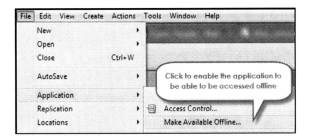

3. We need to select options according to our requirements such as when we want to create the local application. If we select **At the next scheduled replication**, we will need to ensure a schedule has been set up as this is when the replica will be created. If necessary, we can change our schedule and defaults for all local replicas by clicking the **Set or Change Schedules** button.

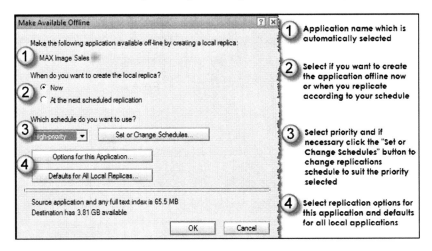

4. Click **OK**. A replica of the application will be added to the **Replication and Sync** page and will begin replication according to when we have selected it to.

Changing and managing locations

We select different locations depending on where we are. We described the different locations earlier in this chapter. Here we discuss how to switch between locations.

There are four options for changing our location:

1. When we log into Lotus Notes, we may be prompted with a login screen. From within this screen we enter our password and select our location.

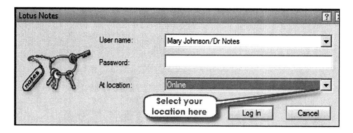

2. If we are not prompted by the login screen, then we may be prompted with a dialog box with a list of locations to select from. Select the location we require and then the **OK** button.

3. If we are currently within Lotus Notes, we can change locations by clicking in the right-hand side of the Status Bar as below in the screen shot or by selecting **File | Locations | Switch Locations**.

4. Select **File | Locations | Switch to Locations**, select the location we require, and then the **OK** button.

Identifying our location in Lotus Notes

There are two ways that we can identify the location we currently have selected:

1. Open our mail, underneath our name in the top left-hand corner, we will see either **on Local** or our home server's name. Typically local means we are working **Offline** (or **Island**), **Home**, or **Travel**. When the server name shows at the top of our mail, it is an indication that we working **Online**.

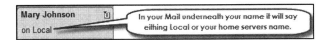

2. In the far right of the status bar, we will see our current location. In the example below the current location is **Offline**.

Creating a location

We may want to create our own location. For example, we may be able to access our office via the Internet at our home but we don't want to use the **Online** location as we would prefer to access our mail and applications locally on our PC. We will create a location document for use when we can access via the Internet.

1. Select **File | Locations | Manage Locations…**.

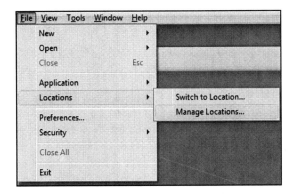

2. Click **New**, the following New Location dialog box will open.

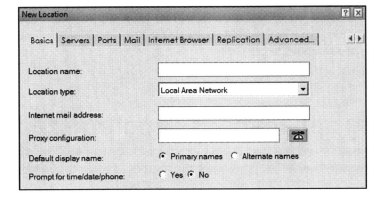

3. Enter a name for the location in the **Location Name** field. In this example let's call the location Internet.

4. In the **Location Type** select an option. In our example select **Local Area Network**.

5. In the next field, **Internet mail address**, we need to enter our internet e-mail address.

6. Select any of the other options that are relevant on the **Basics** tab.

7. On the **Servers** tab, enter **Home/Mail server** name and any other necessary server names. We may need to discuss what server names we need with our IT Department.

8. On the **Ports** tab select **TCPIP**.

9. On the **Mail** tab select **Local** for the **Mail file location**.

10. Go with the defaults for the other field's values or change according to your preferences. Remember **Local** means our local PC.

11. The last option on this tab is **Transfer outgoing mail if XX pending**. I enter the number **1**, which means if I have one e-mail in the Outgoing Mail application it will send that one e-mail. If we enter **2**, then our mail will not get sent until we have two e-mails pending in the Outgoing Mail application.

12. On the **Internet Browser** tab, we need to select our preferred Internet browser.

13. To create a schedule to ensure replicas synchronize within a timeframe, click the **Replication** tab and the tick **Replication is enabled for this connection**. If we have scheduled replication and we become disconnected from our network, Lotus Notes will try to replicate and realize it can't and stop. It will give a message in the status bar saying it cannot find the server. It will not slow down or effect Lotus Notes. I have a scheduled enabled all the time on my Internet location and I use this location even when my network is not available at home.

14. On the **Advanced** tab we can select an ID we want to switch to when we use this location. We may need to change to a different ID and we can use this option to switch to it easily.

15. Once we have finished, click **OK**.

Keeping applications synchronized

Obviously we want to receive our latest e-mails, meeting invitations, and have our applications up-to-date. To do this we must replicate on a regular basis.

Replicating (synchronizing) mail, calendar, and To Dos

Our mail, calendar, and To Dos all reside in the one application. When we replicate our mail we are in turn replicating our calendar and To Dos. The following are the steps we need to perform to replicate mail, calendar, and To Dos.

1. First, we need to open mail.

2. Click the **Send/Receive Mail** icon in the action bar of our messages. Note this icon is only available in a local replica of mail.

3. Alternatively go to the **Replicatiion and Sync** page via the **Open** button.

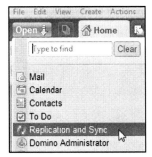

4. Click on the **Start Now** drop down and select **Start Mail Only Now**.

 Even though the button states **Mail Only...**, this type of replication will also sychronize our calendar and To Dos.

Replicating (synchronizing) all applications including mail

Previously we learned how to replicate our mail, calendar, and To Dos. We can replicate all our applications including mail. It is important to keep replicas up-to-date.

1. Click on the **Open** button and select **Replication and Sync**.

2. Click on the **Start Now** button and select **Start Now**.

3. The replication process will replicate each application listed starting at the top of the **Replication and Sync Page** and working down the list. We will see a status of each replication including the number of documents replicated and the time remaining before replication is finished at the bottom of the screen.

4. If required we can stop the replication of the current application and skip to the next application in the list by clicking **Next** at the bottom of the replicator page.

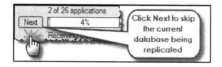

5. When we start replication, the **Start Now** button changes to a **Stop** button. Click the **Stop** button to stop replication if required.

Replicating an individual application

There are times when we may need to replicate only a particular application. We can follow the steps given here to perform this task:

1. Click on the **Open** button and select **Replication and Sync**.

2. On the **Replication and Sync** page, select the application that we want to replicate, then right click. This will show a menu, where we need to select **Replicate Selected Application**.

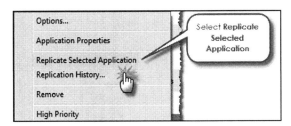

Replicating when shutting down or starting up Lotus Notes

When we start Lotus Notes we can configure Lotus Notes to automatically replicate to prompt asking if we want to replicate. This is configured when we set a schedule, which we will cover next. The prompt asks if we want to **Send data to servers (update servers with changes made to the local applications).** This sends changes made in the local replicas to the replicas on the server. It will also send any changes that were done on the server replicas to the local replicas.

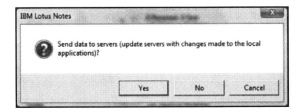

We can:

*   Select **Yes** to replicate
*   Select **No** to not replicate
*   Select **Cancel** to stop shutting down Lotus Notes

Managing replication via the Replication and Sync page

When we view the options available on the **Replication and Sync** page, we can see columns and rows. Each row is an application that has a replica created locally. If we double-click the row, it will open the application; however, typically we will open applications via the **Open** button. The columns show which applications are enabled for replication when they were last replicated along with the number of documents sent and received.

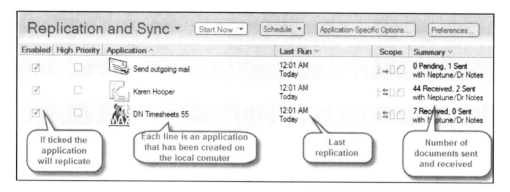

The action buttons at the top of the **Replication and Sync** page enable us to start replication. We can also set specific replication options for individual applications and defaults for all applications by clicking the **Application-Specific Options...** button. We can also create a schedule by clicking the **Schedule** button.

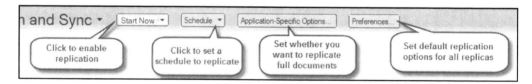

At the bottom of the **Replication and Sync** page, we can see which application is currently being replicated and the time remaining. If we move away from the Replication and Sync page while we are replicating, we can see still the progress in the status bar.

Setting a replication schedule

We have learned how to replicate manually; we can also set a schedule so that replication will occur in the background automatically. This is a great option if we are working from home and we can remain connected. If we have a schedule enabled, we can disable it at any time.

1. Open the **Replication and Sync** page.

2. Click the **Schedule** button and then **Set Replication Schedule...**.

3. Select the options that we require. We can refer to steps 1, 2, and 3 in the following screenshot for more details.

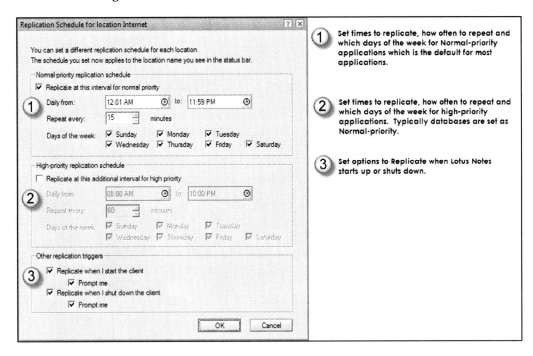

4. Finally, we need to click **OK** to save our changes.

 Note: Each location has its own Replication and Sync page and schedule.

Summary

Working away from the office in this day and age is a common occurrence. In this chapter we reviewed the components that enable us to use Lotus Notes while we are away from the office. We discussed the steps we need to take to ensure our laptop is set up for us to be able to work away from the office. We also explored the different remote situations we can find ourselves in and which location to select. Finally, we learned how to keep our applications synchronized by manually replicating them and how to set up a schedule.

11
Symphony

How often do we have our e-mail application open, then a word editor, perhaps a spreadsheet, and lastly we may be preparing a presentation? We may also want to convert several of these documents to PDF which means we will need PDF conversion software. Typically this would require five applications to be open and we would need to be licensed to use these five programs.

Wouldn't it be easier if all these applications were contained into the one interface? Well, with Lotus Notes we do as we have all these applications combined into one. Within Lotus Notes there is an integrated version of Lotus Symphony, which is IBM's award winning office productivity software that allows us to create documents, spreadsheets, presentations, and it even has a PDF creator.

Lotus Symphony supports the **Open Document Format (ODF)**. ODF is important and valuable because it provides choice, cost effectiveness, and control over the use of our documents and the intellectual property they contain. ODF enables efficient interchange of information between various parts of an organization and between organizations. This is a great asset as we no longer need to worry that a recipient of our documents won't be able to open them.

Obviously in one chapter we cannot explain how to use a word processor, a spreadsheet application, and a presentation application. Instead we will focus on using these applications within Lotus Notes. If we require further information, we can visit the Symphony website by going to `http://symphony.lotus.com/ software/lotus/symphony/home.nsf/home`.

The Symphony version, integrated within Lotus Notes, may be a different version than the version that is currently available. IBM has plans to be able to update Symphony within Lotus Notes; however, at the moment it is not possible. If we require the latest version of Symphony, we can download it from the above website and install it separately. Remember it is free, so we have nothing to lose!

In this chapter we will explore:

- What is Lotus Symphony
- Overview of documents, spreadsheets, and presentations
- Creating documents, spreadsheets, and presentations in Lotus Notes
- Opening and saving Symphony files
- Symphony Toolbar/Menu options, properties, and status bar
- Formatting options
- Template organizer
- File recovery
- Exporting to PDF
- Printing and bookmarking

What is Lotus Symphony

Lotus Symphony is an office productivity suite that allows us to create, edit, and share documents, spreadsheets, and presentations. It is provided free of charge by IBM and can be downloaded and installed as a standalone product; however, we will be exploring the integrated version of Symphony, which is within Lotus Notes. When we install Lotus Notes, we can select to install the productivity tools called Lotus Symphony.

If Symphony has been installed, we will see the options to create **Documents**, **Presentations**, and **Spreadsheets** on the **Home** page as shown here:

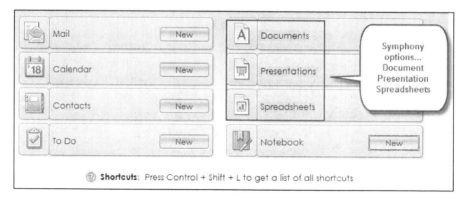

As Symphony provides support for Open Document Format, we can import and edit Microsoft® Office documents and export those documents to ODF for sharing with ODF-compliant applications and solutions. The advantage of this feature is that we are not locked-in to any one vendor's proprietary technology. There are several office suite applications that support ODF, which is important in moving forward as this ensures accessibility and compatibility of our documents.

Documents overview

Documents is the Word processor tool in Lotus Symphony. When we create a document, we can make it as simple or as highly structured as we like. We can add graphics, tables, and charts. We can select from a various array of formatting options such as paragraph styles, the duplicate formatting tool, or font effects. There are a number of features that give us control over the formatting of text, pages, sections of documents, and entire documents. There are also several document templates available. We can visit `http://symphony.lotus.com/software/lotus/symphony/gallery.nsf/GalleryDocuments?OpenView&Count=15` to see the gallery of document templates available.

Spreadsheet overview

When we create a spreadsheet, we are able to perform standard and advanced spreadsheet functions to calculate, analyze, and manage our data. We can visit `http://symphony.lotus.com/software/lotus/symphony/gallery.nsf/GallerySpreadsheets?OpenView&Count=15` to see the gallery of spreadsheet templates available.

Presentation overview

When we create a presentation, we can create a professional presentation that includes charts, drawing objects, and text. We can check out the templates at the IBM Symphony website to fast track our presentation creation. Click here to see the gallery of presentation templates available: `http://symphony.lotus.com/software/lotus/symphony/gallery.nsf/GalleryPresentations?OpenView&Count=15`.

Creating documents, spreadsheets, and presentations

To create documents, spreadsheets, and presentations in Lotus Notes is very simple. We will show the steps to create documents; however, if we want to create a spreadsheet or presentation, we need to follow the same steps except selecting either spreadsheet or presentation.

Follow either one of the steps given next:

- Go to the **Home** page and click the **Documents** icon in the screenshot or click the **New** button.

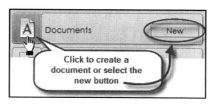

- Select **File | New | Document**.

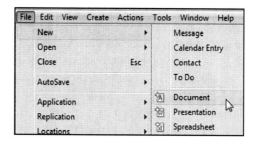

- Click the **Open** button and then select **Lotus Symphony Documents, Lotus Symphony Presentation,** or **Lotus Symphony Spreadsheet**.

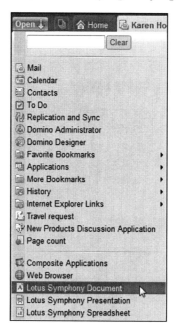

- Select **File | New | From Template | Document**.

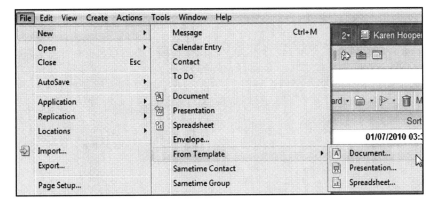

By default the only template files installed with Lotus Notes are presentation templates. We can download template files from `http://symphony.lotus.com/software/lotus/ symphony/gallery.nsf/home` or create our own.

The new document will open as a new window tab in Lotus Notes as circled in the following screenshot:

Opening Symphony files

To open Symphony files, select **File | Open | File** as shown here:

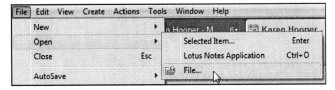

Alternatively to open files that we have recently opened, select **File | Recent Files** and then select the file we require from the list provided.

If we are currently working within a **Document**, **Spreadsheet**, or **Presentation**, we can use the keyboard shortcut of *Ctrl+O* to open another file. If we are in mail or a Lotus Notes database, *Ctrl+O* will open the **Open Database** dialog box.

Saving Symphony files

There are several file formats that we can select from when we save Symphony files.

In the case of **Documents** we have the following choices:

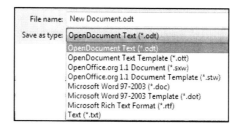

In the case of **Spreadsheets** we have the following choices:

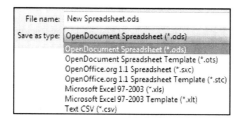

And for **Presentations** we have the following choices:

Symphony toolbar/menu options

As soon as we create a document, spreadsheet, or presentation, we will see new toolbars and menu options. The following is the default toolbar set for documents. Pop-up text describing what each button will do displays when we hold our mouse over the toolbar buttons.

We can add more buttons to the toolbar by right-clicking and selecting **Toolbar** from the right-click menu. In the following screenshot, the blue checked items are currently showing on the toolbar for documents:

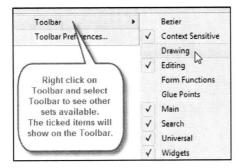

Symphony properties

Properties are available for text, paragraphs, and pages for documents; text and cells for spreadsheets; and text for presentations. To show properties, we need to select **View | Properties Sidebar** and then select either **Float** or **Close.**

Once we have the properties sidebar open, we can change which properties are displayed by clicking the menu option as displayed in the following screenshot:

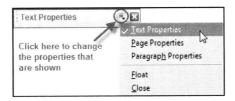

The following screenshot shows the **Text Properties**:

Symphony status bar settings

There are several items that are displayed by default in the status bar, which is positioned at the bottom of the screen above the task bar. We can change what is displayed by selecting **View | Status Bar | Settings**. The following screenshot shows the items that we can select; items that are checked will be displayed.

Formatting options

There are many formatting options available including:

- Predefined styles for paragraphs, characters, and headings
- Inline spell checking and correction
- Graphics that we can insert to create a variety of tables, charts, diagrams, and drawn items
- Automatic creation of a table of contents, indexes, and footers and headers

Symphony shortcuts

There are certain keyboard shortcuts that we could use to make working with Symphony easier. The following table shows those:

Shortcut	Description
Ctrl + N	Creates a new document, presentation, or spreadsheet based on our current opened file type.
Esc	Terminates the action or dialog.
Ctrl + P	Opens the print dialog box.
Ctrl + X	Cuts out the selected highlighted area.
Ctrl + C	Copies the selected items.
Ctrl + V	Pastes from the clipboard.
Ctrl + A	Selects all.
Ctrl + Z	Undoes last action.
Ctrl + Y	Redoes last action.
Ctrl + F	Opens the find & replace dialog.
Ctrl + B	The bold font style is applied to the selected area. If the cursor is positioned in a word, this word is also put in bold.
Ctrl + I	The italic font style is applied to the selected area. If the cursor is positioned in a word, this word is also marked in italic.
Ctrl + U	The underline font style is applied to the selected area. If the cursor is positioned in a word, this word is also underlined.
F11	Opens the style list.

Template organizer

Templates fast track the creation of standard-type documents. We can create our own templates or download them from the Symphony website. Alternatively, we can import the templates that we may already have.

Within Lotus Notes there is a Template Organizer where, as the name implies, we can organize our templates! The Template Organizer works with libraries that are designated folders on our local file system containing template files we can import into the Template Organizer. By default, there are some presentation templates supplied, which reside in the **Default Template Library**.

To view the options of the Template Organizer, we can refer to the following screenshot and perform the steps listed next:

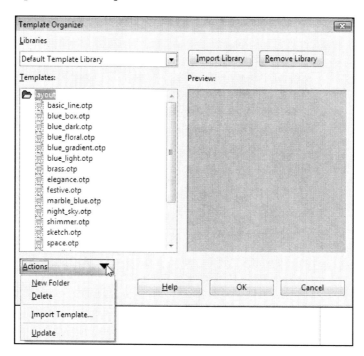

1. Click **File | Template Organizer | Launch**.

2. Click to import a template library to the template organizer. Enter the name and the path of the library in **New Template Library** window.

3. If we want to use a template, we need to select the library it belongs to and then select a template.

4. Click **Actions** to select further options.

   ° **New Folder**: Creates a new folder of templates.

   ° **Delete**: Deletes the file or folder.

   ° **Import Template…**: Inserts the selected template into the selected library.

   ° **Update**: Updates selected templates or template files.

5. Click **OK** when finished.

Creating a presentation from a template in the default library

To create a presentation from the default template library, we need to follow steps listed next:

1. Click **File | Template Organizer | Launch**.

2. Select the **Default Template Library** in the **Libraries** field.

3. In the **Templates** area, expand **layout** by double-clicking on the word **layout**.

4. Select a template; we can preview by clicking on each `.otp` file and viewing them in the **Preview** pane.

5. When we are happy with our selection, click the **OK** button and a presentation will be opened using the template we selected.

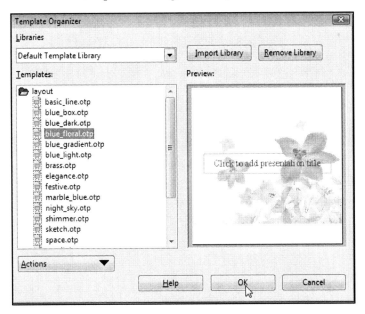

File recovery

When file recovery is enabled, a temporary file is automatically saved for all open files for us to be able to recover these files if the system quits unexpectedly. The default time frame is 10 minutes and it will display nine open files. By default, the **File Recovery** option is enabled; the option can be accessed via **File | Recover**. We can change these preferences by accessing **File | Preferences | IBM Lotus Symphony | File Supervision**.

Exporting to PDF

To export the current document, spreadsheet, or presentation we currently have open into PDF format, select **File | Export**. This opens the **Export** dialog box; from within the dialog box we can select where we want to save the PDF and the filename. The **Export** dialog box is displayed here:

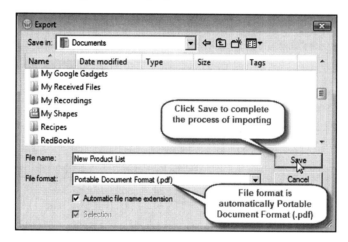

Printing

To print in Lotus Symphony, we need to select **File | Print** or *Ctrl+P*. We can print the current document, a selected area of the document, or pages that we specify. We can also set the print options for the current document. If we want to preview the printed pages, click **File | Print Preview**.

Summary

In this chapter, we have introduced using Symphony within Lotus Notes. Symphony gives the Lotus Notes user many options at no cost. It is versatile as it supports the Open Document Format, which is a standard in today's technology.

If we require further information, we may visit the Symphony website: `http://symphony.lotus.com/software/lotus/symphony/home.nsf/home`.

Conclusion

The end of this chapter concludes this book and I hope that you have enjoyed the journey of discovering the power, diversity, and effectiveness of Lotus Notes. I am passionate about Lotus Notes and have used it for many years; I hope that this book has helped you appreciate all that Notes can do.

We have explored much of what Lotus Notes has to offer from the Home Page to working with Feeds and Widgets. We have learned of the power of Sametime as well as delved in depth into mail, contacts, calendar, and To Dos. We then explored applications, how to work remotely with Lotus Notes, and finally Symphony.

I wish you, the reader, all the best in your endeavor to work smarter and understand Lotus Notes further. I can only hope that what I have presented to you has assisted you and opened you up to all that Lotus Notes has to offer.

To continue the journey of learning, I highly recommend the following website: `http://www.ibm.com/developerworks/lotus/notes`. This is a wiki that has great learning material including tutorials, tips, and examples of Lotus Notes.

Index

Thank you for buying
IBM Lotus Notes 8.5 User Guide

About Packt Publishing

Packt, pronounced 'packed', published its first book "Mastering phpMyAdmin for Effective MySQL Management" in April 2004 and subsequently continued to specialize in publishing highly focused books on specific technologies and solutions.

Our books and publications share the experiences of your fellow IT professionals in adapting and customizing today's systems, applications, and frameworks. Our solution based books give you the knowledge and power to customize the software and technologies you're using to get the job done. Packt books are more specific and less general than the IT books you have seen in the past. Our unique business model allows us to bring you more focused information, giving you more of what you need to know, and less of what you don't.

Packt is a modern, yet unique publishing company, which focuses on producing quality, cutting-edge books for communities of developers, administrators, and newbies alike. For more information, please visit our website: www.packtpub.com.

About Packt Enterprise

In 2010, Packt launched two new brands, Packt Enterprise and Packt Open Source, in order to continue its focus on specialization. This book is part of the Packt Enterprise brand, home to books published on enterprise software – software created by major vendors, including (but not limited to) IBM, Microsoft and Oracle, often for use in other corporations. Its titles will offer information relevant to a range of users of this software, including administrators, developers, architects, and end users.

Writing for Packt

We welcome all inquiries from people who are interested in authoring. Book proposals should be sent to author@packtpub.com. If your book idea is still at an early stage and you would like to discuss it first before writing a formal book proposal, contact us; one of our commissioning editors will get in touch with you.

We're not just looking for published authors; if you have strong technical skills but no writing experience, our experienced editors can help you develop a writing career, or simply get some additional reward for your expertise.

IBM Lotus Notes and Domino 8.5.1

ISBN: 978-1-847199-28-7   Paperback: 336 pages

Upgrade your system and embrace the exciting new features of the Lotus Notes and Domino 8.5.1 platform

1. Upgrade to the latest version of Lotus Notes and Domino

2. Understand the new features and put them to work in your business

Domino 7 Application Development

ISBN: 978-1-904811-06-0   Paperback: 228 pages

Writing and upgrading applications for the latest Lotus Notes Domino Platform

1. Get to grips with all of the major new developer features in Lotus/Domino 7

2. Use DB2 as your Domino data store, optimize your code for performance, adopt best practice

Please check **www.PacktPub.com** for information on our titles

Linux Email

ISBN: 978-1-847198-64-8   Paperback: 376 pages

Set up, maintain, and secure a small office
email server

1. Covers all the information you need to easily set
    up your own Linux email server

2. Learn how to provide web access to email, virus
    and spam protection, and more

IBM Cognos 8 Planning

ISBN: 978-1-847196-84-2   Paperback: 424 pages

Engineer a clear-cut strategy for achieving
best-in-class results

1. Build and deploy effective planning models
    using Cognos 8 Planning

2. Filled with ideas and techniques for designing
    planning models

Please check **www.PacktPub.com** for information on our titles

CPSIA information can be obtained at www.ICGtesting.com
Printed in the USA
LVOW041353170113

316021LV00004B/116/P